Lord, When Did I See You?

Robert L. Pumfery

VANTAGE PRESS
New York

Cover design by Susan Thomas

FIRST EDITION

Published by Vantage Press, Inc.
516 West 34th Street, New York, New York 10001

Manufactured in the United States of America
ISBN: 0-533-14660-7

Library of Congress Catalog Card No.: 2003094080

0 9 8 7 6 5 4 3 2 1

To all those who have inspired me

Contents

Introduction

God has been good to me. As I have been led along the path from skepticism to faith and service, God allowed me to be trained as a scientist and to encounter other faiths before allowing me to become a Christian. God has shown me that religions are not alike. They have some great differences. But there are many, many similarities. That is not surprising. If God is love and God so loves the world, then he loves the person of another faith as much as the Christian. It follows that out of that love God hears the prayers of all and speaks to all. For me Christianity gives the purest insight into the nature of God. But sometimes, perhaps, someone else heard something God said more clealy than did the Christians. Even if not, reflecting on differences can enlighten us on what and why we believe as we do.

I offer the following experiences and comments based on my understanding of primarily two passages of Scripture. The first:

Hebrews 12:1: Therefore, since we are surrounded by so great a cloud of witnesses, let us also lay aside every weight, and sin which clings so closely, and let us run with perseverance the race that is set before us. . . .

I am convinced that we are surrounded by a cloud of witnesses, both people and events, which testify to the content our faith and teach us lessons from our Lord.

The second, from Jesus' Parable of the Sheep and the Goats:

> **Matthew 25:37: Then the righteous will answer him, "Lord, when did we see thee hungry and feed thee, or thirsty and give thee drink? 38: And when did we see thee a stranger and welcome thee, or naked and clothe thee? 39: And when did we see thee sick or in prison and visit thee?" 40: And the King will answer them, "Truly, I say to you, as you did it to one of the least of these my brethren, you did it to me."**

I have discovered that as we minister to those hurting, we encounter the risen Christ and have the opportunity to learn from him.

The titles come not only from the above Scripture but also from the following hymn. Several years ago as I reflected on that Scripture and our past experiences, God was nudging me to be poetic. The words flowed as if I were mere a conduit.

Lord, When Did I See You?

(Sung to the tune of "Battle Hymn of the Republic")

I saw the starving mother with the baby at her breast,
  the gaunt and hungry faces of the children and the rest,
  I tried so hard to help them, Lord, I tried to do my best,
  Lord, when did I see you?

Refrain: Welcome, Christian, into glory,
                  I was there but you did not see,
              That the love you gave to others,
                  Was love you gave to me.

I saw the thirsty people in the good land turned to sand,
   and I heard their cries of anguish as the dry winds parched
      the land;
I paused, O Lord, a moment to reach out a helping hand,
   Lord, when did I see you?   *Refrain*

I saw him shyly standing there, a stranger tall and thin,
   When he seemed to hesitate, unsure, I beckoned him,
     "Come in."
"The Church," I said, "is for us all. Being Christian makes us
     kin."
   Lord when did I see you?   *Refrain.*

I simply gave my jacket to the man out in the cold,
   and I shared a few belongings with the woman, weak and old.
Perhaps I could have served them more if I had been more bold.
   Lord, when did I see you?   *Refrain.*

I visited the prisoners who were locked up in the jail
   and I told them of the Lord above whose mercy would not
     fail.
And of how he'd been a prisoner; that his flesh had felt the nail,
   Lord, when did I see you?   *Refrain.*

I tried to help the sick, O Lord, but, Lord, I don't know how.
   I held a hand or put mine on a flushed and fevered brow,
and prayed for their recovery, Lord, as I am praying now.
   Lord, when did I see you?   *Refrain.*

Lord, When Did I See You?

Genesis

Genesis 12:1: Now the Lord said to Abram, "Go from your country and your kindred and your father's house to the land that I will show you."

The leaf lay in a slight depression at the base of a hill. Even strong winds would not dislodge it, but only cause it to jiggle back and forth. Then the rains came. The individual drops, which struck the leaf, would cause it to tremble, but little else. Farther up the slope, the droplets combined to make a trickle. The trickle joined with others to cause a small flow of water to descend towards the leaf. It in turn coalesced with others, and a small stream was formed. By the time the accumulation found its way to the leaf, it was able to pick it up and carry it away.

God works in our lives in much the same way. No act occurs in isolation. God wanted Abram to go to Palestine. Events got him from Ur to Haran. Then God spoke to him. Possibly it was directly. Initially I would guess it was through others. Maybe a friend said, "Abe, did you hear about the opportunities in a land of the Canaanites?" Maybe a wise sage said, "Abram, you're a bright young man. Don't waste your talent here. Go south to the land of milk and honey and find your blessing." After Abram had thought it over, he probably asked God and God said, "Go!"

My meeting Carole, whom I would marry, was the result of many encounters, events, and relationships for both her and me, which brought us together. Likewise the flow of events from my graduate studies in astronomy, to my discovery of Lunik III

1

on its return from the moon, to going to work for the Smithsonian Institution in the space program, picked up my leaf from where it was securely stuck and thrust me into a strange new and exciting world. It is through many small events and many people that God gets us to "the land that I will show you."

Carole

I Corinthians 12:7: To each is given the manifestation of the Spirit for the common good.

Paul's list of gifts of the Spirit is not exclusive. Carole has what I call the gift of awareness. Her awareness of situations is uncanny. At age three she knew that she would become a nurse, marry a pastor, and become a missionary. When we met, I learned only of the first. When we married, she thought the others were just childish dreams since I was an agnostic astronomer. She told me of the others only after my calls to ministry and mission service respectively. She is aware of health problems within the family, even at great distances. She senses trauma in the lives of members of congregation. "You'd better call on so-and-so this morning" or "Something is happening with the Blank family."

I have learned not to question. Following her awareness, I have often arrived at homes that were in the midst of a crisis and was able to minister to the situation. While your gift or mine might not be spectacular nor mentioned specifically, *to each* is given the manifestation of the Spirit *for the common good.* Cherish and use your gift.

John Hagans

I John 3:18: Little children, let us not love in word or speech but in deed and in truth.

The Rev. John O. Hagans was Carole's pastor when we met and the first member of the clergy I had known. He was wise and gentle and radiated love. Knowing the value Carole placed on church membership, I was motivated to make her happy. I approached John about joining the church. At the time I considered myself an agnostic. There probably was a God, I felt, but I knew it could not be proved. My "membership class" consisted of two questions. "Do you believe in God?" "Yes," I hesitantly answered. "What will you be doing for the Smithsonian?" John asked.

For the next half hour, we talked about my job in the space program. No, I didn't know anything about the Church or the meaning of membership. But as I look back on it, he did exactly the right thing. If he would have pushed or challenged, I would have reacted negatively. His gentle love drew me closer.

Iran

2 Chronicles 36:23: "Thus says Cyrus king of Persia, 'The LORD, the God of heaven, has given me all the kingdoms of the earth, and he has charged me to build him a house at Jerusalem, which is in Judah' "

Before we arrived in Iran, the land of Cyrus and the Persians, we had been filled with many fears of thieves and diseases. Political events kept us from flying from Teheran to Shiraz, our new home. Instead we endured a two-day dusty bus ride in an ancient overcrowded bus filled with people speaking a language we did not understand. Even our overnight stop in Isfahan did not relieve our anxiety.

Upon our arrival in Shiraz, we quickly discovered that the Iranians are wonderful people. As in any country where sanitation is a problem, one learns to use certain caution with raw fruits and vegetables. But we also experienced how delicious is their food. Isfahan quickly became one of our favorite get-away destinations. We learned not to make premature judgments about people and places. All the world is God's world and every people are God's people. They just come in delicious variety.

John White

Matthew 6:7: And in praying do not heap up empty phrases as the Gentiles do; for they think that they will be heard for their many words.

John White had a doctorate in Victorian literature and had worked for many years for the United States government, often in the area of perfecting documents. He gifted me with knowledge about interacting with people, especially by the written word. Although he taught me several ingenious methods to use in correspondence to fight effectively, his greatest help was in **K**eeping **I**t **S**hort and **S**imple.

At the tracking station, we worked from before sunset until after sunrise in teams of two observers. John and I often worked together. As I conducted experiments, I would periodically need to send a memo back to headquarters requesting equipment. I was tempted to expound at length. John would take my document and mark out 95 percent and say, "That's what you want

4

to say and all they want to read." So instead of pages of rationales, my new end product would read, "Am experimenting with . . . please send. . . ." I found that lesson useful in all forms of communication. People often run out of "Listen" before many of us run out of "Talk."

Norman Sharp

Acts 8:31: And he said, "How can I, unless someone guides me?"

In a Muslim country, Friday is the day of rest. Worship at the Church of St. Simon the Zealot was Sunday evening. The pastor was the Reverend Ralph Norman Sharp, a short, slender, balding man in his sixties. He had come to Iran in his mid-twenties and had been pastor of this church for about twenty-five years. He was a scholar and Orientalist. He could read, write and type Farsi, the language of Iran. He served two congregations, the one in Shiraz and one in the village of Qallet. To reach Qallet, he rode his bicycle over twenty miles on gravel roads for the Sunday morning worship, returning to the city in the afternoon for the evening service.

His sermons often reflected events going on around us. Shiraz sits near the intersection of three great tribal migration routes. Nomads pass near the city on their spring and fall treks. At those occasions, we would hear of Abraham coming down out of Haran, the Exodus from Egypt, or the like. Then we would go out and watch the tribes and envision biblical events. The texts of the Bible became alive in the verbal artistry of this talented man. But isn't the task of every Christian to make the Bible visible to others?

Hessam Tavakolian

I John 3:18: Little children, let us not love in word or speech but in deed and in truth.

I was working for the Smithsonian Institution in their satellite tracking program and assigned to Shiraz, Iran. Two of my co-workers were Iranians, Hessam Tavakolian and Hassan Hajeb. Both were physics graduates from the Geophysical Institute of the University of Teheran. Both became our good friends. Although we deeply appreciated Hassan, Hessam became a special person in our lives. From helping us to get orientated to life in Shiraz and teaching us basic Farsi, to finding us an apartment and domestic help, to just being a friend, we could depend on Hessam.

Now that I'm a pastor, I wish I could have a few Hessams in my congregations. If I were to spy a coin lying on the street, Hessam would counsel, "Don't pick it up. God put it their for the needy." Hessam and his family had a modest home in the style of most Iranian homes with a central courtyard containing a small pool and flowers. Since there was plenty of room, Hessam had invited several beggars to camp there.

On one occasion, the observers and wives had gathered at the tracking station to observe a partial solar eclipse. Carole was several months pregnant at the time. Hessam told her, with concern, "During the eclipse, be careful not to touch your stomach. We believe that wherever you touch will leave a mark on the baby." Carole said, "Oh, like this," and touched her stomach three times, a few inches apart. Horrified, Hessam rushed to the Mosque to pray that the results of her foolishness might be lessened. When our son, John, was born, he had three small birthmarks, one each on neck, chest, and heel.

Hessam was deeply devout and unpretentious about his faith. He observed the prayers, the fasts, and the feasts with religious piety. I wish my faith was as strong as his and that all Christians could love in deed and truth as much as my Muslim friend.

Muhammad

Deuteronomy 6:4: "Hear, O Israel: The LORD our God is one LORD."

I was fascinated by the Iranian people and began studying their culture, including their religion. I discovered that the Prophet Muhammad was truly one of the great men of God. Being sensitive to divine inspiration, he spoke out against the idol worship so prevalent in his home town of Mecca. "There is no god but God," became his primary message. Despite extreme opposition, he remained faithful to his calling. Similar to the Jewish faith, his central tenet of faith was that there is only One worthy of worship.

I began to wonder what Christianity would be like today if it had not moved into the world of the Greeks and Romans. There, where the belief was rampant of male gods producing offspring as the result of encounters with human woman, our theology got very sloppy.

Ishmael

Genesis 16:15: And Hagar bore Abram a son; and Abram called the name of his son whom Hagar bore, Ishmael.

Ancient Arab oral tradition differs from ancient Jewish oral tradition. Both remember that Abraham had two sons. The eldest and rightful heir was Ishmael, the son of the Egyptian woman Hagar. Isaac was the son of Sarah and some fourteen years younger. Both traditions agree that Sarah became jealous, had Hagar and Ishmael cast out into the desert, and that God intervened to save their lives. Ishmael was to be the father of the Arab people while his half-brother would become a patriarch of the Jewish people. The Arab tradition says that Abraham was called to sacrifice Ishmael instead of Isaac as a test of faith. It also provides a story of the journey of Abraham and Ishmael to Arabia where they discovered a marvelous black stone and used it to build a place of worship to God. This shrine is called the Ka'ba and is now surrounded by the great mosque in Mecca. Here we have relatives who have different sacred memories of ancient events. I am certainly glad that my memories of past events are better than my wife's, or son's or . . .

S—L—M

John 14:27: Peace I leave with you; my peace I give to you; not as the world gives do I give to you.

Arabic and Hebrew, I was to learn, are sister languages. The similarities are obvious in the greetings. *Salaam aleikum. Shalom aleikum.* Peace be with you. But what kind of peace? Both Hebrew and Arabic were originally written without vowel signs.

Using our script, "Peace" in Arabic would be "SLM" or in Hebrew "ShLM" The depth of this word becomes apparent in the Arabic. The name of the religion is Islam (SLM), meaning "submission" (to God). To designate an adherent, one adds a prefix "Mu." A Muslim (MSLM) is one who has submitted oneself to the will of God. Peace (SLM) is that which comes from God to the adherent (MSLM) when he or she has submitted (SLM) oneself to the will of God. It is inner, spiritual, and has no connection to what the world gives one. *Salaam/Shalom aleikum.* Peace to you!

Allahu Akbar

I John 3:19: By this we shall know that we are of the truth, and reassure our hearts before him. 20: whenever our hearts condemn us; for God is greater than our hearts, and he knows everything.

"Allahu Akbar." Often mistranslated as "God is great," its meaning is "God is greater" and it is the keystone of much of Muslim theology. God is greater than what humans can comprehend. Whatever statement we make about God, it is always wrong because Allahu Akbar. If we say "God is love," we are in error because he is beyond just "love." This is not just good Islamic theology.

The Christian Saint Augustine reportedly told the story of being by the Mediterranean Sea. He observed a young boy with pail and scoop. The child had dug a hole in the sand. He made repeated trips to the sea, filling his pail and emptying it in the hole he had dug. When asked what he was doing, the boy replied that he was putting the entire sea into the hole that he had made. Augustine commented that that is like trying to put the immensity of God into the mind of man. Whatever we have in our thoughts about God, Allahu Akbar, God is greater!

The Quran and the Bible

John 1:1: In the beginning was the Word, and the Word was with God, and the Word was God. 2 He was in the beginning with God; 14: And the Word became flesh and dwelt among us, full of grace and truth; we have beheld his glory, glory as of the only Son from the Father.

God, says the Muslim, has sent many prophets into the world, four of whom carried books. Moses had the Torah, David had the Psalms, Jesus brought the Gospels, and Muhammad delivered the Quran. The content, i.e., submission to God, was the same. In each case, mankind corrupted the carrier's message, making their successor a necessity. Jesus was the greatest. Muhammad was the final prophet. His book, the Quran, is the uncreated speech of God. Rephrasing Christian terms, "In the beginning was the Word . . . and the Word became Book." The Quran is not to be examined. It can only be questioned as to how it is to be put into practice. It has introduced a rigidity and inflexibility into Muslim life and thought. Given in Arabic it ceases to be the Quran when translated into another language.

In contrast, consider the greatness of the Bible. Although divinely inspired, it contains mankind's understanding of how God has been acting in our lives. It might contain passages of varying value, have a wide variety of literary styles, and even have statements that contradict one another, but it has the vitality and freedom to express truths to a variety of cultures over thousands of years. And in it, I began to find "the word (that) became flesh" as interpreted by the New Testament writers.

The Shi'ites

Isaiah 9:7: Of the increase of his government and of peace there will be no end, upon the throne of David, and over his kingdom, to establish it, and to uphold it with justice and with righteousness from this time forth and for evermore.

Islam is divided into two main groups, the Sunnis (Practice) and the Shi'ites (Partisans of Ali). Most of the world's Shi'ites live in Iran, where they are the vast majority of the population. The two groups differ in several ways. Most Shi'ites are Aryans. Most Sunnis are Arabs. The languages are Farsi and Arabic, respectively. But the greatest difference is religious. Christians who affirm that the Messiah had to be a descendent of David will appreciate the Shi'ite side of their conflict with the Sunnis. When the Prophet Muhammad died, he had failed to appoint a Successor (Caliph). The most worthy person was selected, Abu Bakr, close friend and supporter of the Prophet. He in turn by Umar and then Uthman.

The fourth Caliph by this reckoning was Ali, cousin and son-in-law of Muhammad. Ali had married Fatima, daughter of the Prophet. Ali and his eldest son, Hassan, were poisoned. Hussein, Ali's other son, was killed in battle as he attempted to become Caliph. The Shi'ite claim is that succession should be within the family of the Prophet. Ali should have been the first Caliph. Thus Hassan would be second, Hussein the third.

Their argument that the Arabs killed the family of the Prophet brings images of Christians, who claim that the Jews killed Jesus and the hatred both have engendered. I also began wondering about the parallel with those Christians who say that only those with apostolic succession (passed on through an unbroken line from Peter) can officiate at the Lord's Supper despite the spiritual worth of an individual.

Mahdi

Acts 1-10b: Two men stood by them in white robes, 11: and said, "Men of Galilee, why do you stand looking into heaven? This Jesus, who was taken up from you into heaven, will come in the same way as you saw him go into heaven."

The Sunni and the Shi'a branches of Islam can be compared with the Roman Catholic and the Protestant divisions within Christianity with the former in each case being in the majority. Within the Shi'ites, one finds different groups just as there are a variety of denominations within Protestantism. The largest group is known as the Twelvers. They assert that there have been twelve Imam (leaders) beginning with Ali. The twelfth Imam is said to have disappeared mysteriously and his reappearance is awaited. He is the Mahdi, the "hidden one."

The Jews have Elijah, the Zoroastrians have Zoroaster, the Christians have Jesus and the Muslims have the Mahdi. Each is thought to have been taken to heaven by God, and each is expected to return. Is there something inherent in mankind that we need to believe in a hero who, when times are bleak, will come like the cavalry to the rescue?

Baha'u'llah

Romans 2:14: When Gentiles, who have not the law do by nature what the laws requires,. . . . 15: They show that what the law requires is written on their hearts, while their conscience also bears witness and their conflicting thoughts accuse or perhaps excuse them 16: on that day when, according to my gospel, God judges the secrets of men by Christ Jesus.

In 1844 an Iranian Shi'ite by the name of Ali Muhammad declared himself to be the Mahdi and took the name the Bab (the Door or Gate). He was publicly executed in Tabriz in 1850. His message of a new, world faith was carried on by one of his pupils. Husayn-'Ali. Born November 12, 1817 in the city of Shirz, he adopted the title Baha'u'llah, meaning "the Splendor of God." He spent most of his life in exile until he "ascended" in 'Akka in 1892. His followers, the Baha'is, number in excess of five million around the world. Since a primary emphasis among his teachings is "all the prophets of God proclaim the same faith," many of the Baha'i houses of worship have nine sides with a door in each. This symbolizes the belief that there are nine major religions through which mankind may come to God. They believe in universal education, racial and gender equality, and promoting peace. For them prayer, meditation, and work done in the spirit of service to humanity are expressions of the worship of God. I hope for the best for both them and us when God judges the secrets of men by Christ Jesus.

Sufi

2 Corinthians 12:2: I know a man in Christ who fourteen years ago was caught up to the third heaven—whether in the body or out of the body I do not know, God knows. . . . 4: and he heard things that cannot be told, which man may not utter.

As far as I know, Hinduism is the only faith that spells out specifically that there are three approaches to God—by faith, by works, and by experience. We are all acquainted with the first two and probably find both within us. The tension between them is expressed in James with "faith without works is dead." The third is to encounter God in a mystical way. Within Islam, those who go this route are called the Sufis. The origin of their name is lost but may be derived from the wool garments they wore. The best known of the Sufis are the Dervishes who through mantra-style chants and spinning movements in dance try to induce a trancelike state.

Christians might do it through meditation, praying the Rosary, or speaking in tongues. It is not an either/or proposition. However we might realize the presence and love of God in our lives—by knowledge, by deeds, or by mystical experience—we have the company of saints of all religions.

Jinn

Isaiah 13:20: It will never be inhabited or dwelt in for all generations; no Arab will pitch his tent there, no shepherds will make their flocks lie down there. 21: But wild beasts will lie down there, and its houses will be full of howling creatures; there ostriches will dwell, and there satyrs will dance.

Especially in the desert wilderness dwell creatures called the jinn. The Jewish Talmud says that they are an intermediate order between angels and humans. In Arab thinking, they are spirits that often lead humans astray in matters of faith, much like New Testament demons. For the Iranians, they can be mischievous and troublemakers like imps, gremlins, and other Western folk-creatures. Occasionally the power of the jinn has been appropriated.

The story from *The Thousand and One Nights* of the jinni in the bottle is an example. However, some have become Muslims. They were impressed by the Sufi and took interest in their prayers and dance. If you go out on a hot summer day and see the small whirlwinds we call dust devils, it is just one of the jinn whirling in dance and praising God.

Satan

Deuteronomy 4:35: To you it was shown, that you might know that the LORD is God; there is no other beside him.

Job 2:10: But he (Job) said to her (his wife), "You speak as one of the foolish women would speak. Shall we receive good at the hand of God, and shall we not receive evil?" In all this Job did not sin with his lips.

How we deal with the problem of good and evil depends on our presuppositions. For Christians, we assume that since God is good, God cannot be the source of evil. We also assume that it must be other than mankind, because you and I can't be to blame. Therefore, there must be a third source, whom we name Satan from which evil is generated. This results in God apparently being unable or unwilling to prevent Satan from performing evil acts. If unable, God is not all-powerful and Satan thus becomes a god, albeit minor and lesser. If God is unwilling, then God's goodness comes into question.

For the Muslim, their Creed begins, "There is no God save God." God is neither "good" nor "evil" in the human sense. God is greater. God is in control and either allows events to happen or prevents them. Whether we perceive something as good or evil is essentially our problem. It is what God wills. I suspect that the early Jewish and Christian faiths were both closer to this concept of evil than the one we now hold.

Hell

Matthew 25:41: Then he will say to those at his left hand, "Depart from me, you cursed, into the eternal fire prepared for the devil and his angels. . . ."

Isn't it interesting that for the five great religions that originated in the hot and arid region of the Middle East—Zoroastrianism, Judaism, Christianity, Islam, and Bah'ism—the place of torment is also a locale of eternal heat. Would an Eskimo prophet describe hell as a place where one shivers and chatters the teeth? Hot or cold, these physical images suggest the literally most God-forsaken place. Eternal absence from the presence of God is a pain beyond description.

Call of the Muezzin

Daniel 6:10b: and he got down upon his knees three times a day and prayed and gave thanks before his God, as he had done previously.

The lingering memory of most people who have lived in a Muslim land is the call of the muezzin. Five times a day (sunset, night, dawn, noon, and afternoon) he mounts the minaret of the mosque. In a powerful voice and to a cadence and tune that has been set for ages, the faithful are called to prayer. In Arabic he cries, "God is greater. There is no God but God, and Muhammad is the apostle of God. Come to Prayer. Come to Security. God is greater."

And the devout Muslim prays those five times. At the mosque, or at home or at work, or at the roadside, wherever he might be. He stops what he is doing and offers his prayers to God.

I loved the sound of the call to prayer. It reminded me also to stop what I was doing and give thanks to God.

Qibla

Matthew 5:14: You are the light of the world. . . . 16: Let your light so shine before men, that they may see your good works and give glory to your Father who is in heaven.

Every Muslim in prayer is to turn toward the Sacred Mosque in Mecca. To mark the Qibla, the direction of prayer, each mosque has one wall that is distinctive. It usually also contains a niche for candles or a lamp to aid the worshipper at night. Even in a dark world, by seeing the light, the individual knows where to direct his prayers and praise. Isn't that also our task? We are called to exhibit the light so that others might direct their thanksgiving to God.

Ablutions

II Corinthians 7:1: Since we have these promises, beloved, let us cleanse ourselves from every defilement of body and spirit, and make holiness perfect in the fear of God.

In every mosque and in an obvious place is a source of water. It might be a huge bowl near the entrance or a pool in the courtyard. Before a Muslim may bow in prayer, he or she must complete the ritual ablutions. After the practice of the prophet Muhammad, they wash the hands, mouth, nose, and nostrils, face, arms, head, ears and feet. It is a symbolic cleansing of what they have said, heard, thought, been, and done before they enter into conversation with the Holy One. What preparations do we make before we enter into conversation with the Holy One. What preparations do we make before we go to the Lord in prayer?

Prayer Postures

Mark 11:25: "And whenever you stand praying, forgive, if you have anything against anyone; so that your Father also who is in heaven may forgive you your trespasses."

Have you noticed how we worship? Other than standing for some hymns and certain Scriptures, we sit comfortably in our seats. I am old enough to remember when even Methodist churches had kneeling benches in the pews. They were removed because of disuse. We worship basically with our minds. When my Muslim friends pray, they do so with their entire body. There are times when they stand as the Jews did in Jesus time.

God deserves the respect as the King, the Judge, the Revered One. They bow from the waist to the Ultimate Royalty. They sit to listen to the Great Teacher and prostrate themselves in utter submission to the All Powerful. The body language influences the mind. It can help remind us of just Who we are worshipping.

Hands

I Timothy 2:8: I desire then that in every place the men should pray, lifting holy hands without anger or quarreling;

If we do anything with our hands during worship, it is to clasp them with palms together in a begging gesture. Our Muslim brothers and sisters assist their prayers with many uses of the hands. They place them alongside the ears so as to hear God better, upwards to praise the God in heaven, outward to receive the gifts God is offering, etc. We use hand gestures when talking with other friends. Why not with our Best One?

Prayer Beads

Psalm 111:4: He has caused his wonderful works to be remembered; the LORD is gracious and merciful.

Sharing of religious practices is probably as old as mankind. Design of places of worship, methods of prayer, and concepts of the divine flow from one people to another. As one walks through the streets of any Muslim city, one is reminded of this by the prayer beads that many men carry. Arranged in three sets of eleven beads, with separators between adjacent sets, these beads assist the worshipper to remember the ninety-nine beautiful names of God (the Merciful, Compassionate, . . .).

Where these beads originated is anybody's guess. The Muslims apparently acquired the practice from the Hindus after their invasion of India. They passed it on to the Roman Catholics as the two faiths interacted in Spain. The latter called it the Rosary. Although called by different names and accompanied by different prayers, the function remains the same. It is to aid the devotional life of the one who carries and uses it.

Universality

Acts 2:46: And day by day, attending the temple together and breaking bread in their homes, they partook of food with glad and generous heart.

Other than the Friday sermon, which is in the vernacular, all of the obligatory prayers are prescribed and in Arabic. This means that any Muslim, Sunni, Shi'ite or Sufi, from any country and speaking any language, may worship fully in any mosque in the world. Is it any wonder that they look askance at our fragmentation and discriminations?

The Persian Carpet

Matthew 5:48: You, therefore, must be perfect, as your heavenly Father is perfect.

Carole and I decided we should buy a Persian carpet. Our friend Hessam agreed to go with us to the bazaar and assist us. The process was itself interesting. Sitting amongst the carpets and holding a sugar cube between one's teeth, we sipped strong tea and listened to the business and family woes of the seller. He said he would like to lower the price, but. . . .

As we looked at a multitude of carpets, it became apparent that even the best carpet had an obvious flaw, perhaps a thread of the wrong color or a misshapen pattern. We asked Hessam about it and were told that the flaws were deliberate. You see, only God is perfect. It would be pretentious and trying to put oneself on a par with God if one were to attempt to make a perfect carpet (or anything else). Therefore, the errors are noticeable and intentional.

Interestingly, many Christians aren't bothered by the thought that they are trying to be on a par with God.

Inshallah

James 4:15: Instead you ought to say, "If the Lord wills, we shall live and we shall do this or that."

Inshallah, "If God wills," is a frequently used phrase through most Muslim lands. Inshallah. If we come or go, if we are happy or sad, if we live or die, it is all directed by the will of God. This is often viewed by foreigners as either fatalism or as a handy excuse. In the former, it seems as if the Muslims believe that we are completely at the mercy of outside forces with little responsibility of our own. In the latter, the customer, for example, sees it as a cop-out. The store clerk's "Your order will be ready tomorrow, Inshallah," is interpreted to mean "Don't hold your breath."

The Muslim, however, recognizes that we do have choices and responsibilities. However, God is in control. God may or may not allow that which we have intended. Recognizing that fact, the adherent to Islam is saying, "I intend to do such-and-such, however, God will determine if that is the case." Do we believe that God regulates our activities or can we do whatever we wish without God's involvement?

An Almost Common Creed

I Timothy 3:16: Great indeed, we confess, is the mystery of our religion: He was manifested in the flesh, vindicated in the Spirit, seen by angels, preached among the nations,, believed on in the world, taken up in glory.

Many of us have memorized that ancient catechism known as the Apostle's Creed. For some, it is surprising that the Muslims would agree with most of its contents. The Muslim would probably edit it as follows:

I believe in God, Almighty, creator of heaven and earth,
and in Jesus Christ, who was born of the virgin Mary,
suffered under Pontius Pilate and was crucified.
He ascended into heaven, is seated at the right hand of God,
and will come again to judge the living and the dead.
I believe in the Spirit of God, the forgiveness of sins,
the resurrection of the body, and the life everlasting.

Jesus, they hold, was the greatest of the prophets and the bearers of books to mankind. He was too good to have been the victim of evil men. That would have been a defeat for God. The other book-bearers (Moses, David, and Muhammad) all died of wonderful old age. So they maintain that although Jesus was crucified, at the last minute God provided a substitute. Jesus was taken alive into heaven where he awaits his return to earth for the time of judging. Many suggest that it was Judas Iscariot who took Jesus' place on the cross and perished there. Difference with us, yes. But I would be willing to bet that there are many devout Christians who have more points of difference with the Apostle's Creed than do most Muslims.

Lent and Muharram

Luke 9:21–22: "The Son of man must suffer many things, and be rejected by the elders and chief priests and scribes, and be killed, and on the third day be raised." 23: And he said to all, "If any man would come after me, let him deny himself and take up his cross daily and follow me."

Is it a characteristic of mankind to want to enter into the suffering of one's hero, especially of spiritual matters? The Christian Church has long had a season known as Lent in which we participate in the suffering of Jesus. For forty days prior to Easter, not including Sundays, Christians are urged to pray, fast, do sacrificial acts, and reflect on the final days of Jesus' life. In some locations, individuals actually allow themselves to be crucified.

A similar situation is found with the Shi'ite Muslims. On the tenth day of the first month of the year, according to the Arabian calendar, the month of Muharram, Hussein, son of Ali and Fatima and grandson of the prophet Muhammad, died in battle near the town of Karbala. Since his father and brother predeceased him, this line of descendants ended in this event. But the Shi'ite faith had its birth.

In Iran, Muharram is known as the "month of mourning" with the first ten days being especially important. Passion plays are produced. Sacred processions are held with flagellants beating themselves with devices made of several foot-long chains attached to a wooden handle. In former days, knife blades were affixed to the chain ends. The flagellation is in unison as the participants and crowd chant, "Hus-sein, Hus-sein". . . .

Whether in the observance of Lent or Muharram, I wonder if our spiritual leaders might repeat to modern followers the words Jesus said to his apostle, Phillip: "Have I been with you so long, and yet you do not know me?" (John 14:9a)

Jihad

I Timothy 6:12: Fight the good fight of the faith; take hold of the eternal life to which you were called when you made the good confession in the presence of many witnesses.

We have been led to believe that Jihad, "Holy War," means fighting against non-Muslims. In a sense it does, but only if one expands the usage. Jihad means the exerting of one's power in repelling an enemy. The enemy could be an invading army, or it could be unbelievers and scoffers within one's community. A jihad could even be against those within your religious body who are resisting doing the will of God.

On a personal level, the enemy can be the one who is tempting you. It is also the human nature within you, which is keeping you from fulfilling your potential. The "mujahidin" are those who struggle hard in keeping the faith. Paul's advice to Timothy and to us is similar. We must be involved in the struggle to keep the faith at all levels.

Hostages

Luke 4:18: The Spirit of the Lord is upon me, because he has anointed me to preach good news to the poor. He has sent me to proclaim release to the captives and recovering of sight to the blind, to set at liberty those who are oppressed, 19: to proclaim the acceptable year of the Lord.

During the "crisis" when the Americans were taken hostage at the Embassy in Teheran, I was asked my opinion concerning their safety. My reply was simple. There is nothing to worry about as long as the captors are truly Islamic fundamentalists.

Islam forbids the killing of women, children, the elderly and members of the clergy. Also, the Quran specifically states that after hostilities have ceased, all prisoners must be either released as a favor or be allowed to be ransomed. The killing of hostages is reprehensible to God.

An illustration of this comes from the Crusades and the struggle between Richard the Lion Heart and Saladin. Richard captured the city of Akka and demanded a ransom. When it was not paid on time, the Christian king ordered twenty-seven hundred Muslim captives to be slaughtered.

Contrast this with Saladin, who after taking Jerusalem, released a thousand Christian hostages at the request of his brother as something pleasing to God. Another thousand were let go on an appeal by the patriarch. The remainder of his captives Saladin set free as his gift to the Almighty. Muslims take the teachings of the Quran very seriously even in war. I wonder what it would be like, if all Christians would as conscientiously follow the teachings of Jesus?

Mediation

Matthew 16:16: Behold, I send you out as sheep in the midst of wolves; so be wise as serpents and innocent as doves.

To whom do you go for advice or mediation? In 1 Kings 12, Reheboam, Solomon's son, picked that of his friends and contemporaries rather than the elders who had advised his father. The result was a split in the kingdom. In the Iranian hostage situation mentioned above, the United States went to its ally Saudi Arabia to intercede with the fundamentalists. It was an act lacking in wisdom.

First, doing so would be like asking the Pope to mediate with an independent fundamentalist Protestant group. Second, the worst name you can call an Iranian is an "Arab." It is considered more derogatory than "pig" or "dog." The world is full of wolves. Without using the wisdom that God offers, doves simply end up as a meal.

Harem

I Peter 3:7: Likewise you husbands, live considerably with your wives, bestowing honor on the woman as the weaker sex, since you are joint heirs of the grace of life, in order that your prayers may not be hindered.

The word "harem" brings all sorts of images to the Western mind of palaces filled with women and the like. The word means "sacred and forbidden." The women's apartments and their occupants are harem to men other than the husbands. What was intended to keep women safe has tended to keep them restricted. When entrusted with the well-being of another —spouse, child, enfeebled parents, other—it is difficult to keep the balance between their protection and their freedom.

Chadoor

Leviticus 19:15: You shall do no injustice in judgment; you shall not be partial to the poor or defer to the great, but in righteousness shall you judge your neighbor.

The chadoor is the one-piece garment worn by Muslim women that covers them from head to ankles. It is condemned by those women who have fine clothing that they want to display, those who have attractive figures, and those who can afford variety. It is a blessing to those who cannot afford a variety of clothing, the poor whose clothing beneath the chadoor is tattered and torn and to those who have unattractive bodily features. Wouldn't it be wonderful if we judged another by who they are rather than how they appear?

Polygamy

I Timothy 3:2: Now a bishop must be above reproach, the husband of one wife, temperate, sensible, dignified, hospitable, an apt teacher, 3: no drunkard, not violent but gentle, not quarrelsome, and no lover of money

Where it has been allowed, polygamy has been practiced only by the small minority who could afford more than one wife. Islam allows up to four wives, provided one treats them equitably. Polygamy was practised in the early Church and was not outlawed until several centuries after Christ. Since we cannot have more than one wife at a time, many Americans practice sequential polygamy, having several wives but not simultaneously.

Status

Proverbs 31:30: Charm is deceitful, and beauty is vain, but a woman who fears the LORD is to be praised.

Generally, in most Islamic societies, the status of a woman is not measured by her faith or personal qualities, but by the family, wealth, and/or occupation of her husband. Beyond that, the first wife has a higher status than the second. A wife who bears children is more highly esteemed than one who is childless. One who bears sons is respected more than one who gives birth to only daughters. The highest ranked is she who has the most sons. Sure sounds familiar!

The Flautist

Isaiah 30:39: You shall have a song as in the night when a holy feast is kept; and gladness of heart, as when one sets out to the sound of the flute to go to the mountain of the LORD, to the Rock of Israel.

God acts in strange and wonderful ways to grant us blessings. One evening in Shiraz, I had the night off. Carole was working at Nemazee Hospital. John had not yet been born, so I was alone. Our second-floor apartment was still hot from the day's heat, so I wandered out on our balcony to enjoy the cool night air. I sat there in the darkness listening to the voices being carried on the night air, the distant bleating of sheep and goats, and the tinkling of their bells being accented by the occasional deeper throated chime of one worn by a camel.

Some time had passed when I noticed an older black Mercedes make its way slowly up our street and stop at the three-way intersection some fifty yards from where I sat. Two men got out of the four-door sedan, removed a small carpet the size of a prayer rug, and spread it on the corner sidewalk. Returning to the vehicle, they lifted a legless man from the back seat and placed him on the carpet. They then returned to the car and disappeared down the street.

My attention turned to the figure seated just across from me. Slowly he lifted a flute to his mouth and began to play. The music was indescribably beautiful. Clear, resonant tones drifted on the night air. No angel of heaven could have produced sweeter sounds. It seemed like only moments had passed, but my watch told me that it had been more than an hour, when the car returned. The ritual was repeated in reverse fashion, and I was left with a treasured memory. I never met the flautist, nor did I hear or see him again. But he is still with me, especially on cool summer evenings, as I sit in the darkness. I hear his melodies, and thank him and thank God. May we all be attuned to the serendipitous blessings God puts into our lives.

Noruz

Ecclesiastes 3:1: For everything there is a season, and a time for every matter under heaven: . . . a time to keep, and a time to cast away.

The greatest national holiday in Iran is Noruz, a new year's celebration. Noruz occurs on the vernal equinox and the beginning of spring. The animals—sheep, goats, camels and donkeys—receive liberal splashes of dye, mainly reds and blues. In the evening, there is partying, with singing and dancing. Dried vegetation resembling heavy two to three foot diameter tumbleweeds are arranged in piles. The mounds are then set ablaze.

Since the kindling point is low, the fire is bright but not very hot. Folks then run and jump the line of fires. As they do so, they receive blessings. Wishes will be fulfilled. Unmarried girls will find a husband. Childless women will become pregnant. Pregnant women will receive sons, etc.

The custom goes back to ancient times and a long-forgotten celebration of a god, Yima, "whose glance is like the sun." The celebration of Noruz has survived the reforming efforts of the Zoroastrians (from the sixth century B.C.), the Christians (from the second century A.D.), and the Muslims (from the seventh century A.D.). None with any success. Perhaps this is the source of the phrase, "We have always done it this way." The task is in knowing what one should keep and what should be discarded.

Dr. Mehra

Psalm 8:3: When I look at thy heavens, the work of thy fingers, the moon and the stars which thou hast established. . . .

It was shortly after the close of the International Geophysical Year, the eighteen-month scientific cooperative endeavor collecting data about the earth. Since Shiraz had been one of the research centers, a director of the organizing body arrived to express appreciation. Civil leaders from the city and members of the foreign community met at the Iran-American Society for the event. We gathered in a compound with nothing but the cloudless heavens for a roof. The host for the evening, Dr. Mehra, director of Namazi hospital, introduced the speaker who expressed gratitude for local efforts. Part way through his speech, he paused.

Looking up at the sky, he said, "I am a physicist by training. When I see the stars, I see spectral lines." (Spectral lines are those identifying lines that appear when a beam of light has passed through a gas and then has been broken down into a rainbow by a prism.) He then finished his lecture.

Dr. Mehra then arose and thanked him for coming to Shiraz. Then he added, almost apologetically, that he had to differ with the speaker on one point. "When I see the stars," said Dr. Mehra, "I hear poetry." Both men were products of the twentieth century and scientifically trained but from extremely different cultures. Imagine then the mistakes we present-day Westerners must make when we try to project our ideas and concepts on people who are from the ancient, pre-scientific Middle East. People like Moses or David or Jesus.

The Yazdi

Ezekiel 37:10 The hand of the LORD was upon me, and he brought me out by the Spirit of the LORD, and set me down in the midst of the valley; it was full of bones.

One day in Shiraz, I visited an art show in one of the local banks. An oil painting caught my attention. On the left side of the canvas was a valley seen as if by x-ray vision. Buried beneath the soil were human bones scattered in disarray. As the eye moved toward the right, the landscape moved gently upward. At the base of the hill, the bones were protruding out of the soil. Farther up the slope, the bones were gradually assembled into skeleton form. Near the peak they were clothed with flesh and were walking toward the sun. I stood for some time with my attention riveted on the scene before me.

An Iranian man about twenty years of age approached me. He was a student at the University of Shiraz and the artist. My knowledge of the Bible was poor, but I had heard the song "Dry Bones." "Ezekiel?" I asked. "Avesta," he replied. He was a Zoroastrian from Yazd, he explained. The Avesta is their holy book.

Purchasing two books on the Zoroastrians at the Anglican book store, I gradually pieced together a fascinating sequence. When the Jewish people were taken into Exile by the Babylonians in 581 BCE, they believed that their God was the source of both good and evil. Satan was an angel and agent of God. All humans, at death, descended to Sheol for their sleep through eternity.

The Babylonians were, in turn, conquered by Persians under Cyrus the Great. The Jews had new rulers. The Persians were followers of Zoroaster, and his teachings were to influence the Jewish thought. In the Zoroastrian creation story, a cosmic struggle exists between the all-good god, Ahura Mazd, and the all-evil god, Ahriman. Ahura Mazd traps Ahriman in the earth. The final victory is assured, but the end is delayed. Ahura Mazd cannot approach Ahriman directly. His goodness would be compromised. Having with him celestial but mortal beings with life-spans of a few centuries, Ahura Mazd offers them an opportunity for immortality. They must come to earth and fight Ahriman for him. Many agree. But they (we) tend to forget their (our) allegiance. In time, the victory will be won. Then the dead will be raised. There will be a judgment. Those who failed to fight Ahriman will be punished. Those who were loyal to Ahura Mazd will go on to Paradise.

When the Jews finally returned to their homeland, their religion had changed. They now talked about the struggle between God and Satan, a resurrection, judgment, paradise and hell. Ezekiel could draw upon a story of a valley of dry bones, which was already familiar to his listeners and put a new twist to it. The Zoroastrians had been a source of insight for the Jewish people, eventually for all Christians, and for me. I thank the young man from Yazd for enlightening me with his painting, and I thank God for putting us together.

Fatima

Mark 10:52: And Jesus said to him, "Go your way; your faith has made you well."

As an agnostic scientist, I did not believe in faith-healing. Then I heard of a case that made me reevaluate my position. A ailing man was brought in to Namazi Hospital. This was a fine modern teaching hospital, with many American doctors and nurses on staff and financial support from the Ford Foundation. After the appropriate tests and x-rays, the individual was diagnosed as having an advanced case of tuberculosis and was immediately transported to the Lung Hospital just north of the city. He had been there but a few days, when, while sleeping, he had a vision of Fatima, the daughter of the Prophet Muhammad. She said that, because of his faith, he had been cured. Awaking, he discovered the T.B. symptoms were gone.

After much pleading, he was taken again to Namazi Hospital and reexamined by the same doctors. There was no sign of the disease. His faith had made him well! I wonder if the operative agent was human faith or does God heal those who have faith, regardless of how they worship or by what name God is called?

Queen Elizabeth II

Luke 16:31: He said to him, "If they do not hear Moses and the prophets, neither will they be convinced if someone should rise from the dead."

It was early in 1961 when the word, a rumor at first, started circulating. The Queen of England was coming on a visit to Iran. As time went on, it became definite. Yes, she was coming. Later we learned that she was going to visit Shiraz. Then, she would be here on a Sunday and attend worship at the Church of Simon the Zealot. It was said that admission would be by invitation only. The normal attendance on Sunday evening began growing. From the usual 12 or 13 persons, we had 20, 25, 30.

The day of the queen's visit finally arrived. The church was packed with over 200 persons. Prince Philip read the Scriptures. Rev. Sharp was eloquent, as usual. It was a marvelous event.

The next Sunday was Easter, the Day of the Resurrection. Only 60-some persons were at worship. Then 30. 20. Well before Pentecost, we were back to the usual handful of worshippers. The message was obvious. To most persons,, the presence of a Queen is of more importance than the resurrection of the crucified Lord.

Earthquake

Zechariah 14:5: And the valley of my mountains shall be stopped up, for the valley of the mountains shall touch the side of it; and you shall flee as you fled from the earthquake in the days of Uzziah king of Judah.

A few weeks earlier, there had been an earthquake nearby. The village of Lar was located at the base of a cliff-face, which crumbled and crushed the homes. Hundreds were killed. I was at the tracking station the night when the earthquake struck Shiraz. The walls of our main building tilted ten or fifteen degrees and then righted themselves. "We just had an earthquake," I said to my partner and went back to work.

When I got home the next morning, Carole was furious with me. The effects of the quake were far more pronounced in our second-floor apartment. The streets had been filled with frightened and screaming people. Why didn't I come home to check on her? I learned a lesson. Just because you are doing well in a traumatic situation does not imply that others are comfortable also.

An Unknown Sufi

Deuteronomy 16:21: "You shall not plant any tree as an Asherah. . . ." 2: Kings 23:7c: ". . . . where the women wove hangings for the Asherah."

Since we were photographing the artificial earth satellites, clear, dark skies were preferable. Shiraz was selected because of its geographic location and its exceptionally clear skies. It was only between mid-November and mid-March that there were any clouds in the sky. The humidity was seldom out of the single digits. Still there were nights that we hoped for the non-existent clouds.

A couple of hundred yards below the station and near our road was an outcropping of rock. The face of it had been painted black, and from its center, a small tree struggled for life. On closer inspection, pieces of cloth could be seen tied to the branches of the tree. In the evening, lighted candles would be placed in the crevices of the stone. Usually there would be five or six. In Muslim reckoning, each day began at sunset. Since Friday was the holy day, on Thursday evening we would see a dozen or more candles adorning the rock.

Years before, a wandering Sufi, a Muslim mystic and holy man, had passed that way. He had paused at that site and rested against the rock. The village folks believed that some of his aura, his holy presence, had remained behind. Thus it became a place of worship and prayer. Requests to God were offered and candles lit. Sometimes, the petition required time for God to answer.

For example, a woman asking for a son. On the first occasion, she would tie a loop of cloth around a branch. The next month, a second would be attached to the first. As time went on, a woven chain would appear. When the request was answered, the chain would be removed and a candle lighted. Since folks assured us that it worked, we were tempted to try it in our hopes for clouds. It became easy to see why the ancient Jewish people became attracted to the Asherahs (sacred poles or trees) for whatever might be their needs or desires.

Manna

Exodus 16:19: And Moses said to them, "Let no man leave any of it (manna) till the morning." 20: But they did not listen to Moses; some left part of it till the morning, and it bred worms and became foul; and Moses was angry with them.

On one of our trips to Isfahan, we were wandering through the over two-miles of covered bazaar and stopped at a sweets seller. He was making a kind of candy called "Gaz," which was made from flour, rose water, and manna. Since his English was good, we talked with him at length about how they gathered the manna. Obviously, our knowledge of the Moses story was lacking, because we asked him for a small amount of manna as a souvenir. We placed it in a film can and took it with us.

Several days later we looked at our prize. It was a melted, sticky, smelly wormy mess. We threw out both can and contents. Moses was right. If you don't use it, you lose it!

Isfahani Beggar

John 5:6: When Jesus saw him and knew that he had been lying there a long time, he said to him, "Do you want to be healed?"

Some of the most beautiful mosques in the world are in Isfahan. In olden times, it was said that "all roads lead to Isfahan." Even a brief visit to this lovely city quickly tells one why that should be true. Even today, many people make their way to this central Iranian city. At the time we were there, one could expect to see a beggar with a case of elephantiasis and sitting on the sidewalk near the Shah's mosque. The thumb of one hand was almost as large a person's forearm. Each day he would greet passersby with calls of "Bakhsheesh" (alms).

The Anglicans had a small congregation in Isfahan with a church and small hospital. A surgeon from the hospital offered to correct the man's problem free of charge. The man refused. He explained that he had a wife and family. They barely made ends meet. However, what he earned by begging was more than what he could possibly make if he were cured. He couldn't afford it. Sometimes, the question "Do you want to be healed?" is followed by the answer, "No, thank you."

Isfahan Synagogue

Ezra 1:2: "Thus says Cyrus king of Persia: The LORD, the God of heaven, has given me all the kingdoms of the earth, and he has charged me to build him a house at Jerusalem, which is in Judah 3: Whoever is among you of all his people, may his God be with him, and let him go up to Jerusalem . . . and rebuild the house of the LORD. . . ."

Isfahan had twelve synagogues. The Jewish community traces its roots back to the Exile. Their ancestors opted to stay in Persia rather than return to Palestine. After all they had their homes and jobs and friends. Besides, why go back to Palestine to serve God. They could worship him and serve him anywhere!

A Man, Woman, and Donkey

Mark 14:7a: "For you always have the poor with you."

It was in Iran that I first encountered the truly poor, those without the ability to climb out of their present situation. It was illustrated by the following story, which circulated at the time.

A traveler came across the scene of an accident. A vehicle had struck and killed a woman and a donkey. Her husband was weeping inconsolably. The traveler tried to comfort the man. "Don't weep," he said, "you will get another wife."

The stricken man replied, "Yes, I know I will get another wife. But I will never be able to afford another donkey." It is hard for us who are rich to understand the plight of the multitudes who are poor.

Right Hands

Matthew 5:30: And if your right hand causes you to sin, cut it off, and throw it away; it is better that you lose one of your members than that your whole body go into hell.

Where people eat with their hands, customs develop as to clean and dirty hands. Probably because most people are right-handed, that is usually considered the "clean hand." It is used to dip into the common food pot, to pass a "clean" object, or to bless another. The left hand is the dirty hand. It is used to feed an animal, pick up dung, or cleanse oneself after defecation. It is a gross act to dip into the food with the left hand. Using the left hand to pass food stuffs to another is a major insult.

The Arab practice of cutting off a thief's right hand is a double punishment. It reduces one's ability to defend oneself, and it sentences that thief to social isolation at meals for the rest of the thief's life.

Jesus says that even when most social contacts come around the evening meal, it is better to lose your right hand and live like a hermit than to lose your soul.

Gatch

Mark 2:4: And when they could not get near him because of the crowd, they removed the roof above him; and when they had made an opening, they let down the pallet on which the paralytic lay.

Our main building at the tracking station was constructed of standard mud-brick called "gatch." The dark room had a problem. The summer daytime temperatures easily exceeded one hundred degrees, and the walls retained the heat throughout the night. The preferred temperature of the chemicals for processing the film is about 68 degrees. We compensated as best we could, but the quality suffered. Obtaining an air conditioner, we surveyed for the best location. The exterior walls were about eighteen inches thick, while the interior ones were only about ten. While there were disadvantages in having the compressor in the office, it would also reduce the chance for vandalism.

We were familiar with gatch and held it in low esteem. It was obviously inferior material. We therefore allotted half a day for the installation. We cleaned the area and got to work with picks and sledgehammers. The first blow produced a dent, which was insufficient to hold a b-b. Blow followed blow. It took two days of hard work to make an opening large enough for the air conditioner. I gained a profound respect for gatch and new insights into the friends of the paralytic. They were willing to dig through the concrete-like material of a roof to lower him so that Jesus might heal him. We should all have such friends!

Shepherds

Matthew 25:31: "When the Son of man comes in his glory . . . then he will sit on his glorious throne. 32: Before him will be gathered all the nations, and he will separate them one from another as a shepherd separates the sheep from the goats. . . ."

The basic color of the Iranian landscape was brown. Everything was brown. The rugged hills, the walls, and the villages were all brown. Because of the blowing dust, even the sparse vegetation was brown. Against this the shepherds with their flocks seemed almost out of place. The shepherds, usually in dark clothing and carrying a stick, would be surrounded by thirty or forty animals. The goats were black or white or mottled and moving briskly from place to place. The fat-tailed sheep had coats ranging from almost pure white, through the browns, to nearly black, and seemed reluctant to exert much effort at all. It was extremely rare to see a flock of only sheep or only goats. Both made up one flock. They followed and obeyed the one shepherd.

That is the setting of Jesus' parable. It is not because the goats followed someone else that they are rejected. Both the sheep and the goats recognize and call Jesus "Lord." Both are parts of the Good Shepherd's flock. In the parable, goats are easily distinguishable from sheep by both their appearance and actions. So are the people.

Ghanat

Psalm 1:1: Blessed is the man who walks not in the counsel of the wicked . . . but his delight is in the law of the LORD. . . . He is like a tree planted by streams of water, that yields its fruit in its season, and its leaf does not wither. In all that he does, he prospers.

By the time of Cyrus the Great (559–530 B.C.), the arid country-side of Iran was marked by an extensive irrigation system known as ghanats. To get water from the mountain streams down to the cities on the plains without losing most of it to evaporation, a series of holes were dug, each about fifteen feet deep and separated from the adjacent ones by twenty or twenty-five yards. Horizontal tunnels were then dug, which connected the bases of the holes. The water would flow essentially underground for miles from the source to its destination. Because of years of neglect, tunnels have collapsed, leaving open ditches with small streams of water.

From the air, even the ghanat systems which are in good repair, are an easily visible line of dots. From the land, it is only those that have broken down that are easily spotted. Vegetation has sprung forth along their banks. The constant supply of water keeps the grass green and the shrubs and trees healthy even in the midst of desert-like surroundings. Villagers will often transplant a favorite tree to such a site.

Such is the image in this Psalm. The person who trusts in God is tenderly transplanted from their parched setting to one where the streams of living water keep them refreshed and fully alive. Are we willing to be uprooted, mentally, physically, socially, and/or spiritually, by God and placed somewhere else?

Winnowing

Psalm 1:4: The wicked are not so, but are like chaff which the wind drives away.

We were riding near the ruins of Persepolis when we passed through a small village. Near the road, a man and a woman were winnowing grain. The wheat had been cut by hand and gathered into a large pile. A stake had been driven into the ground at the center of the mound. Five cows had been yoked together and tied with a long rope to the stake. The cattle proceeded to walk around and around the stake. In the process, they loosened the grain from the stalk. Periodically, the man would retrieve the loosened grain and place it in a new pile some distance away. The straw was put aside for later use. Taking a broad tined pitchfork, the man would toss the grain into the air. The grain, being heavier, settled quickly back to earth. However, the chaff, the husk that had surrounded the kernel, was light. The wind caught it, and in a matter of seconds, it was gone. Puff! And it was no more. When it was sufficiently winnowed, the woman would gather the grain into sacks to take it to the mill. The grain and straw were useful and were saved. The chaff was of no value and dissipated. Just as in the parables.

Compliments

Matthew 12:34b: For out of the abundance of the heart the mouth speaks. 35: The good man out of his good treasure brings forth good, and the evil man out of his evil treasure brings forth evil.

In English, there is a saying, "Beauty is in the eye of the beholder." And while containing an element of truth, it often implies that the object in question is really not that attractive and the seer is somehow deluded. We often heard a similar but richer version.

When an Iranian is complimented, the usual reply is, "Your eyes see beautiful." Because of the goodness inside you, you see things in a better light. May our eyes see beautiful!

Hospitality

Hebrews 13:2: Do not neglect to show hospitality to strangers, for thereby some have entertained angels unawares.

Hospitality became a sacred obligation throughout the Middle East in ancient times. Inns were virtually non-existent. Travel was dangerous. The lack of food and water could be life-threatening. While hospitality has diminished in its intensity, it is still practiced. Strangers are welcomed into homes. Refusals can be interpreted at insults.

And the wise visitor quickly learns not to verbally admire an object in his host home. It might become a gift. Has the abundance of possessions and the fear of losing them caused us to turn aside potential angels?

Forgiveness

Matthew 6:14: For if you forgive men their trespasses, your heavenly father also will forgive you.

It is almost impossible not to offend others, especially in a cross-cultural situation, either by commission or omission. It may be deliberate or unintentional. Excuse me, we say. Pardon me. Forgive me. I'm sorry. And how do we respond? That's all right. You're forgiven. The Iranian will say, "Khoda babakhshid," "May God forgive you," implying that they already have.

Prohibitions

Leviticus 11-7: And the swine, because it parts the hoof and is cloven-footed but does not chew the cud, is unclean to you.

The Quran, like the Old Testament, prohibits the eating of pork. Most meat eaten in Iran is, facetiously, "lamb, ram, ewe and mutton." A shop on the main street of Shiraz was run by an Armenian named Mishel. Inside the store was a u-shaped counter. To the right were canned goods, other grocery items, and the cash register. To the left, was a meat slicer where Mishel made wonderful ham sandwiches. The bread was similar to that used in submarine sandwiches. It was about eight inches in length and sliced horizontally. It was then filled with layers of sliced ham and sliced dill pickles. Then Mishel wrapped them in past issues of an Armenian newspaper. What a delicious treat! Christians would enter, move immediately to the left and order their sandwich.

We soon noticed other customers. They would enter, go to the right side, and whisper to the shopkeeper. Mishel would go around to the opposite side and make one or more sandwiches. Instead of the normal wrappings, these were placed in brown paper sacks. Mishel would return to the cash register and receive payment. The container would then be partially or totally concealed by their clothing as the customer exited the shop. Before I am too quick to criticize, I have to ask myself how often I ignore what is printed in our Book.

Squash

Genesis 1:29: And God said, "Behold I have given you every plant yielding seed which is upon the face of all the earth, and every tree with seed in its fruit; you shall have them for food."

What shall we have for food—the plants, the trees, the fruit, the seed, or all of the above? Near a village we saw a large field filled with harvested squash, similar in size, shape and color to pumpkins. A man and two women were sitting in the midst of them doing something. We stopped our vehicle and approached them. The man was using a short, hoe-like tool to split the squash in half. The women were scraping out the seeds and discarding the fruit. We learned that the seeds would be sold to a firm that would then roast and salt them for consumption in the movie theaters.

We thought, what a waste of good squash. When we offered to buy one, they insisted we simply take one. Carole used part as a vegetable for our meals and the rest for a pumpkin-like pie. Both were delicious. Both we and the Iranians probably thought the others' food choices were strange. As they say, "One man's trash is another man's treasure," or "One man's food is another man's garbage."

The Monkey House

Judges 12:5: And the Gileadites took the fords of the Jordan against the Ephraimites. And when any of the fugitives of Ephraim said, "Let me go over," the men of Gilead said to him, "Are you an Ephraimite?" When he said, "No," 6: they said to him, "Then say Shibboleth," and he said, "Sibboleth," for he could not pronounce it right; then they seized him and slew him at the fords of the Jordan.

Most languages have sounds that are difficult for a foreigner to pronounce. One of those in Farsi, which gave me a problem, was a guttural "kh." I came close, but not close enough. One night I caught a taxi and instructed the driver to go to the Park Hotel. The word for "hotel," literally guest house, starts with that sound. The driver roared with laughter. I had said, "Monkey House Park." I joined him, knowing my mistake.

When we stopped laughing, he took me to my destination. Fortunately, I could laugh at myself. It could have been embarrassing. The event reminds me of the difficulties people of other languages have with pronunciation of English. May I only laugh with them.

Gestures

Acts 13:51: But they shook off the dust from their feet against them, and went to Iconium.

Most people know that words can convey a variety of meanings. Added to this, is the problem of tone, volume, and context. A message heard can be very different than the one intended. Gestures can also provide difficulties. An acceptable gesture in one culture may be obscene in another. In America, nodding the head up and down means "yes," turning it from side to side is "no." In Iran, the way to indicate "no" is by a quick snap of the head upwards. A click of the tongues means the same thing. When combined, it says "absolutely not."

An American friend related how she stood along a busy Iranian street, seeking to hail a taxi. Having been raised in New York City, as a cab approached, she would snap her head upwards in the hailing gesture she had leaned back home. To her dismay, each taxi that had slowed would quickly speed away. Unknowingly, she was sending the wrong signals. I try to be careful with words I use. But I wonder how often I send a non-verbal message that contradicts my intentions.

Satellites

Psalm 8:3: When I look at thy heavens, the work of thy fingers, the moon and the stars which thou hast established; 4: what is man that thou art mindful of him, and the son of man that thou dost care for him? 5: Yet thou hast made him little less than God, and dost crown him with glory and honor.

Having worked in astronomy both before and after the advent of the space age, I have felt a personal change of emphasis in this Psalm. Before 1957 and Sputnik I, everything in the night sky was made by God—the stars, moon and planets. Everything!

Verses 3 and 4 jumped out at me. The uniqueness of God's work is unmistakable as contrasted with the insignificance of humankind. But now when you go out and look up, it is not long before you see a manmade satellite creeping slowly across the heavens. God is the great Creator, but he has made us God-like. Our objects in space do not compare with God's, but they appear and move together with God's.

Gift

Matthew 2:11: and going into the house they (the Magi) saw the child with Mary his mother, and they fell down and worshipped him. Then, opening their treasures, they offered him gifts, gold and frankincense and myrrh.

Our son, John, was born in Shiraz. He was only a few days old when Hessam came by our home. He brought a gift for our newborn son. It was a small gold Iranian coin minted in the year of John's birth. It was an ancient tradition, Hessam said. As long as John kept it, he would never be without resources. Ancient tradition?

The wisemen who visited Jesus are thought to have come from Persia, modern Iran, bringing with them gifts. Gold so he would never be poor, incense so he would never be unable to worship, and myrrh so that he could meet the conclusion of his life successfully. What are we saying symbolically with the gifts we give to God's children that he places in our lives?

Rain

Matthew 5:44: But I say to you, Love your enemies and pray for those who persecute you, 45: so that you may be sons of your Father who is in heaven; for he makes his sun rise on the evil and on the good, and sends rain on the just and on the unjust.

There is a wonderful saying among the Iranians and the Arabs, which needs no comment: "All sunshine makes a desert."

Paradise

Genesis 2:8: And the LORD God planted a garden in Eden, in the east; and there he put the man whom he had formed. 3:8a And they heard the sound of the LORD God walking in the garden in the cool of the day. . . .

In Shiraz, there were several old estates, the palaces of khans. The dwellings reflected the beauty of former days, with mirrors, painting and carved marble figures. But the gardens were especially impressive, completely surrounded by a high wall, which separated it from the arid surroundings beyond it, the gardens were complete with streams and pools, fruit trees and cypress, gardenias and roses. Each was literally a paradise.

"Paradise" is a Persian word, meaning a "walled garden," like those described. In ancient days, it was a great honor to be named the "companion" of the garden. One was invited to walk with the king in the garden in the cool of the day. The pleasure was not in the setting but the presence of the king. When God invites us into Paradise, it is much the same thing. The joy is not in the beauty of our surroundings but in walking with God in the garden in the cool of the day!

Wailing

Mark 5:38: When they came to the house . . . (Jesus) he saw a tumult, and people weeping and wailing loudly. 39: And when he had entered, he said to them, "Why do you make a tumult and weep? The child is not dead but sleeping."

We have all witnessed on the television the wailings of grief by Middle Eastern women. There are even professional wailers who assist the mourners with their grief. How therapeutic when compared to our "Don't cry" and "Get hold of yourself."

Burial

Mark 15:46–16:1: And he bought a linen shroud, and taking him down, wrapped him in the linen shroud, and laid him in a tomb. And when the sabbath was past, Mary Magdalene . . . bought spices, so that they might go and anoint him.

Many of the Muslim customs of burial are similar to those of Jesus' time. The body is washed, wrapped in a shroud, and ointments applied. Even with modern techniques of embalming, burial takes place the day of death if possible. Following a brief service, the body is placed in the grave in fetal position and face directed towards Mecca. In our older churches and cemeteries, people always faced east and toward Jerusalem. I guess it doesn't matter anymore?

Persepolis

Psalm 143:5: I remember the days of old, I meditate on all that thou hast done.

History came alive for us at Persepolis. This southern capital of the ancient Persia was about an hour's drive out of Shiraz. Begun by Darius the Great around 518 BCE and continued by Xerxes I, Artaxerxes I, II, and III, the city was destroyed by Alexander the Great in 331 BCE. Walking between the ancient walls covered with depictions of court life and gazing at the towering pillars, I wondered had Ezra or Nehemiah walked these streets? Was the lion's den of Daniel near here? Since royalty alternated between summer and winter palaces of Susa and Persepolis, did Esther and Mordecai live here? And to think that the God who was so prominent in their lives, cares about you and me today!

Graven Images

Exodus 20:4: "You shall not make for yourself a graven image, or any likeness of anything."

The seventh-century Arabs who conquered Persia believed with the Jews in the prohibition of graven images. At Persepolis, the artwork, which was above the ground, was literally defaced. Fortunately, much was protected by the accumulated sand. The Iranians are not as strict but have shied away from human representations. Ample use in artwork is made of flowers, trees, and birds. As with the Arabs, the mosques have been decorated with beautiful stylized calligraphy using words from the Holy Quran. With the advent of photography, movies, and television, the prohibition against graven images is slipping further into the background. Soon they may catch up with us in our disregard of the second of the Ten Commandments.

Be Ready

Matthews 24:44: Therefore you also must be ready; for the Son of man is coming at an hour you do not expect.

I am an amateur photographer and enjoy taking pictures. John White and I had worked all night. Dawn was breaking when he called me outside. The sun was edging over the horizon in the east. But the beauty was in the west. There two adjacent mountains were made scarlet by the rising sun. The sky in the depths of the vee between them was a deep purple, but gradually was transformed into crimson near their tops. Framed in the depression was a golden full moon.

We stood there in silence as the moon gradually disappeared and the growing dawn washed out the colors. Neither of us had a camera. We didn't expect something like that. We weren't ready. Jesus warns us, that the hour we would be called home would be sudden and unexpected. Whether it is in photography or in living, we better be ready. We never know when. . . .

Crocus

Isaiah 35:1: The wilderness and the dry land shall be glad, the desert shall rejoice and blossom; like the crocus, 2: it shall blossom abundantly, and rejoice with joy and singing.

For a few days in January, the desert is transformed. The water from the winter rains seeps deep into the earth. Almost like a miracle, the crocus springs forth. The arid wasteland is transformed with a carpet of flowers. Out of curiosity, I tried to dig up a crocus. After about five feet, I gave up. The bulb was hidden much deeper.

God does things like that. God hides something precious deep down inside and it persists despite the droughts. And then, at the right time, God provides the moisture, which causes it to burst forth and transform our wasteland.

Reforestation

Deuteronomy 11:16: Take heed lest your heart be deceived, and you turn aside . . . 17: and the anger of the LORD be kindled against you, and he shut up the heavens, so that there be no rain, and the land yield no fruit, . . .

The area near Persepolis was once heavily forested. Through the centuries the trees had been cut and the region assumed a desert-like appearance. Clouds were visible only from November through March. Rain was restricted to December, January, and February. Humidity was in the single-digits.

During 1961, the Shah began a program of reforestation. In large selected areas, saplings were planted. Women with kerosene cans hung on yokes across their necks made the rounds twice a day, pouring a dipper-full of water on each young tree. Armed guards protected the trees with orders to shoot.

In April of 1974, we stopped in Iran on our way home from the Philippines. Our son, John, had been born in Shiraz and was an Iranian citizen, a status that is irrevocable. We wanted him to visit the country of his birth before reaching the twelve years old draft age. He had seen our slides and heard our stories. Consider his and our surprise when we were greeted by large white clouds and even a brief rain shower. In April! The climate had changed.

Is denuding the land of trees equivalent to a sin for which God will withhold the rain? Was reforestation a form of repentance or just good ecology? Or both?

Radical Changes

Nehemiah 13:30: Thus I cleansed them from everything foreign, and I established the duties of the priests and Levites, each in his work; 31: and I provided for the wood offering, at appointed times, and for the first fruits. Remember me, O my God, for good.

The changes in climate due to reforestation weren't the only ones we noted when were returned after eleven years. When we had left Shiraz, the airport building was the size of a double garage set along a single runway and located several miles across an open expanse from the city. The road reaching it was a two-track dirt road. It had been replaced by a large, marble building, more resembling a palace than a terminal. A four-lane divided highway, the median filled with roses, lead to the city.

Three things caught our attention. First, religious observance had declined radically. Many mosques were closed. Few persons offered the prescribed five-times daily prayers. Second, the former sexual mores had changed. The chedoor, the enveloping women's garment, was seldom seen. The prohibition against even casual sexual contact had given way to mini-skirt-clad teenage girls walking hand in hand with a boy friend, carrying a boom box blasting Western music. The third was the invasive presence of American products and way of life. It was everywhere one looked. In only eleven years, the old ways were thrown out and new, foreign ones adopted.

We knew even then that something must happen. The Ayatollah Khomeini was simply walking in the footsteps of the prophets of old. Do we not all need someone who periodically calls us back to the roots of our faith?

Spies

Matthew 10:29: Are not two sparrows sold for a penny? And not one of them will fall to the ground without your Father's will.

We had known that many Iranians who worked for or with foreigners were on the Shah's payroll as spies. They kept records of where we went, what we did, and with whom we did it. We also knew that many of them talked openly with each other. In fact we would make a game of it. During mid-day I might ask one of our drivers about an American friend. He might relate that according to our friend's driver they had gone to so-and-so's home. Their host's maid had said that they ate such-and-such and did this-and-that.

We had assumed that our maid Zahra was a spy and also knew no English. For almost two years,, we struggled to communicate in Farsi. On the day of our departure, she said to us, "Good-bye, Ma'am and Sir. Have a safe journey." Whether it is spies or God, if you are doing nothing wrong, it doesn't make any difference if you are being watched.

Conversion

Isaiah 43:19: Behold, I am doing a new thing; now it springs forth, do you not perceive it?

By the time we left Iran, I was different. Through people of faith, God had introduced me to the wisdom and insights of the Muslim and Zoroastrian faiths. Through people of faith, God opened Christianity to me. Through experiences in the Middle East, God had awakened in me an awareness to new dimensions of human life. After that, God allowed me to become a Christian. But I was not the kind of Christian that I might have become if I had been deprived of those learning. I was aware that God continually does new things in our lives.

South Africa

Galatians 1:15: But when he who had set me apart before I was born, and had called me through his grace, 16: was pleased to reveal his Son to me. . . . I did not confer with flesh and blood, 17: nor did I go up to Jerusalem to those who were apostles before me, but I went away into Arabia; and again I returned to Damascus.

Paul after his conversion did not go out immediately, but had time for preparation. I was a new Christian and needed to grow in the faith. God directed us to South Africa so that which was planted within me could grow. The fruit would come later. Whether in agriculture, the life of an individual, or in ideas and faith, the process is similar. The seed is planted. Gestation occurs, followed by birth. Then comes the maturing process. It is only then that it/we can bear fruit.

Donald Cragg

I Corinthians 2:12: Now we have received not the spirit of the world, but the Spirit which is from God, that we might understand the gifts bestowed on us by God.

It was Monday afternoon. We had been in our home in Johannesburg for two days and it was the first time I had met the Rev. Mr. Donald Cragg. I had attended the nearby church the previous morning and heard a lay pastor. Carole had stayed home with our son, thirteen-month-old John, and went to the evening service. She had met Donald then. The Sandringham Methodist Church seldom had visitors, let alone two Yanks in one day.

Near the close of our lengthy visit, he asked about our future. I mentioned a possible career change to teaching or the ministry. His eyes lit up. Donald explained to us the British Methodist system. Tonight, he said, there was to be a Local Preachers meeting, and he would propose me for the beginning stage. Before I could object, he was out the door. That night I became a Local Preacher. What had he seen that prompted him to act as he did? What a blessing it would be if we all could see the latent gifts that God has placed in someone else and then help to draw them out.

Christmas Party

Deuteronomy 19:19: And you shall teach them to your children, talking of them when you are sitting in your house, and when you are walking by the way, and when you lie down, and when you rise.

It was Christmastime. Carole and I had been working with the Sandringham youth group. They and the youth from the Orange Grove Church had prepared gifts and snacks for a party for the Sunday school children of a church in a black township. At the appointed time, about a dozen of our youth, Rev. Cragg, Carole, our son, and myself arrived at the site. For the children to be allowed to attend, they needed perfect attendance for the past year. Over one hundred children qualified. They had lined up by grades and were singing carols.

Everyone was enjoying the day. Everyone except a little girl who must have been about two years of age. She cried and cried. The church's pastor tried to console her to no avail. He finally ascertained the problem. To get her to behave, her mother threatened her. She would give her to the white people, and, everyone knew, white people ate black people! Seeing us, the child was certain that her end had come.

The play *South Pacific* has a song that states that "you have to be taught to be afraid" of people who are different. We adults have an opportunity. We can implant fear and bigotry and hatred into the innocent minds of children or we can teach and show them about God and love, peace and joy.

Red Letter Edition

Matthew 5:17: "Think not that I have come to abolish the law and the prophets; I have come not to abolish them but to fulfill them."

In one way or another, all of my co-workers at the tracking station helped me in my journey of faith. One day our station chief, who happened to be Jewish, showed me a copy of the New Testament that he had received. It was a red-letter edition with a difference. Instead of indicating the words of Christ, those passages, phrases or concepts that came from the Old Testament were in red. Close to two-thirds of the book was in red print. We do not do well when we overlook our Jewish heritage.

Names

Genesis 32:27: And he said to him, "What is your name?" And he said, "Jacob." 28: Then he said, "Your name shall no more be called Jacob, but Israel, for you have striven with God and with men, and have prevailed."

I was quickly put straight as far as terminology by our white neighbors. Even though they were born and raised in South Africa, they were "Europeans." The "Natives" were black South Africans, even if they were born and raised elsewhere on the continent.

Therefore, many natives were not called "Natives" and many who were not natives were called "Natives." Strange. I'm glad that when we become Christians, we don't have to worry about designations. God changes all of our names to "brothers and sisters."

Apartheid

Matthew 7:3: Why do you see the speck that is in your brother's eye, but do not notice the log that is in your own eye?

While we were in South Africa, apartheid was still government policy. The word "apartheid" in Afrikaans means "apartness." The concept is separate development. It ensures that each culture, group or section of society can retain its cultural uniqueness and heritage. Wherever it occurs, it is interesting that the "concern for protecting another people's heritage" has always come from the groups with the social, political, and economic power.

The two major white segments of South Africa had quite different approaches to the black individual. The Afrikaaner farmer would say to the black worker, "I am superior and you are inferior. As long as you understand that, we can be friends. Come, let's have a beer together." The English approach would be, "You and I are equal. But you can stay over there in your equality and I shall stay over here in mine." I wonder what mental and verbal games you and I play to justify our prejudices.

Classification

Matthew 7:3: Why do you see the speck that is in your brother's eye, but do not notice the log that is in your own eye?

Under apartheid everyone was classified according to race. There were "whites," "blacks," "Asians," and "coloured." The latter meant anyone of mixed race regardless of degree. Apparently someone was doing some research into family histories amongst the Afrikaners. In the Dutch Reformed churches were records of marriages, births, and deaths from the earliest days of the settlement. Some of the mothers listed had strangely African-sounding names. Mysteriously, all of the records disappeared from all of the churches. Undoubtedly we should be hesitant before we judge or "classify" others.

Sin

John 8:7: And as they continued to ask him, he stood up and said to them, "Let him who is without sin among you be the first to throw a stone at her."

We often heard the comparisons between South Africa and our own country (between the former U. of S.A. and the U.S. of A.). Both were colonized by people from northern Europe seeking religious freedom. In both cases, the settlers arrived at the coast and traveled inland by covered wagons. Both encountered aboriginal peoples with whom difficulties arose.

In America, the situation was remedied by virtually exterminating the Indians. In South Africa, the solution was apartheid. Don't we all play that game? I can't be so bad because your sin is worse than my sin.

American Apartheid?

Acts 10:28: and he (Peter) said to them, "You yourselves know how unlawful it is for a Jew to associate with or to visit any one of another nation; but God has shown me that I should not call any man common or unclean."

When informed that Carole was pregnant with her second child, her mother hurried next door to her neighbors. "Carole is bringing home an African baby," she exclaimed.

For the next few minutes, she was subject to a tirade about how a black person in the neighborhood would bring down property values, be a public disgrace, etc. When the objections slowed down, Carole's mother said calmly, "I don't see why Carole and Bob's baby should be black."

Mine Dances

John 13:35: By this all men will know that you are my disciples, if you have love for one another.

Gold mining is a major industry in the Johannesburg area. Thousands of workers are employed. Most of them are blacks from several nations and many different tribes. Each mine compound has a dance arena. Each Sunday one of these is open to the public. Miners perform the dances of their tribe. It is done in a sense of friendly competition. More importantly it promotes pride and identity. Although programs are printed listing the order of presentation, one quickly learns to recognize the distinctive characteristics. That one is Zulu. That's Ndebele. That's . . . I wonder how often someone said of you or of me, "That person is a Christian. I can tell by how they act."

Hungry Children

Mark 10:14: But when Jesus saw it he was indignant, and said to them, "Let the children come to me, do not hinder them; for to such belongs the kingdom of God."

Ironically near Edenvale, "the valley of Paradise," was a shanty-town of squatters who had illegally come to Johannesburg to seek their fortune. Everyone was extremely poor. During the day most adults were in the city either working or seeking employment. The children were left to fend for themselves. Some Catholic women had set up a feeding station. Each day they would offer a peanut butter sandwich and pint of milk to the children. The children had to bring their own container and a one-cent coin.

As Christmas approached the crew at the tracking station decided to buy oranges for all of the children. Since I was delivering the fruit, I was allowed in to what was normally a restricted area for whites. I can still see the hovels of cardboard, sticks, and galvanized roofing. A barbed-wire fence was erected outside the distribution area. Well before the time to receive the food hundreds of poorly clad hungry children were lining up. A little girl remains riveted in my consciousness. She was about seven years old, obviously malnourished and wearing only an ill-fitting dress. On her back she carried a small boy. She had no container or coin. With longing eyes she gazed through the fencing while others received food and ate.

With all of our wealth in the churches of America, apparently we are willing to allow the millions of children like her to be part of the kingdom of God but not part of the world of the well-fed.

Swazi Boy

Proverbs 13:22: A good man leaves an inheritance to his children's children, but the sinner's wealth is laid up for the righteous.

We had stopped to visit a Methodist mission compound in Swaziland. There was a church, school, and small hospital. A doctor gave a tour of the latter. He paused at the bedside of a small boy, perhaps three years of age. The boy's mother had brought him in suffering from parasites and severe malnutrition. Every day she visited her son as he was nursed back to health.

One day she was told that he would be discharged on the following day. She never returned. She knew that as long as he was at the hospital he had a chance for life, which would be denied him at home. She gave him the best gift she could. Would I be so loving?

Nora

John 4:27: Just then his disciples came. They marveled that he was talking with a woman, but none said, "What do you wish?" or, "Why are you talking with her?"

Jewish men had a prayer that was offered each morning: "Thank God that I am not a woman, a Gentile, or a slave." At times, the attitude in South Africa toward black women seemed similar. Nora worked for us, helping Carole with household tasks and child care. The government had classified her as "colored," meaning a person of mixed heritage. One of her grandparents was white, while the remainder were black. She had the equivalent of tenth-grade education and had once hoped to become a nurse. Nora was literate in many South African languages and often was "letter writer" for less fortunate friends. Despite the fact that she and Carole quickly became best friends, Nora was always careful to refer to us as "Master" and "Madam." This was to protect us all from government charges.

If Carole and Nora were to go somewhere together, they could walk side by side or both ride in the front seat of the car. If Nora were to go with me, neither of those were permissible. In a car, I would drive, while Nora would sit in the rear. Nora would eat with us, other than when we had company and accusations could be made. While Carole could legally hug our friend, I could not.

God must weep when governments or religions or societies decide who one may or may not treat with respect and Christian decency.

Bride Price

Genesis 34:12: "Ask of me ever so much as marriage present and gift, and I will give according as you say to me; only give me the maiden to be my wife."

John, a Zulu, lived with Nora in the room behind our house. They were partially married. In Zulu custom, the man is to pay a "lobola," bride price, to the father of the bride to compensate him for the loss of a worker.

In most black societies in South Africa, the vast majority of the agricultural work is done by women. The loss of a daughter can be an economic burden. After partial payment, there is a ceremony and the couple lives together. After a son is born, the remainder of the lobola is paid and the couple is wed.

John had made the initial payment and they had lived together about thirteen years. They had a daughter, Monica, who was eleven. Nora and Carole were both pregnant about the same time. When asked if she hoped for a girl or a boy, Nora told us that she had mixed feelings. If it were a boy, then she and John could finally be married in the church. But, she added, according to Zulu custom, she would be forced to go and live in John's ancestral home, Kraal, in Zululand, with John's other two wives. He would be able to visit them only one month a year. She would be third in line in sharing their husband. It is not only in America that the social rules for men and women have obviously been made by males.

Murder

Galatians 5:19: Now the works of the flesh are plain: fornication, impurity, licentiousness, 20 idolatry, sorcery, enmity, strife, jealousy, anger, selfishness, dissension, party spirit, 21 envy, drunkenness, carousing, and the like. I warn you, as I warned you before, that those who do such things shall not inherit the kingdom of God.

John did custodial work at one of the downtown apartments. He shared dwelling quarters on the top floor with other workers and visited Nora when possible. With the birth of Tamba, Nora's son, he knew his life was changing. When the marriage was completed, Nora would be leaving Johannesburg for his Kraal and he would be without female companionship eleven months out of the year.

John's search for a new girlfriend did not take long. Soon he was giving her gifts so as to cement her affection for him. But he was soon caught in a bind. He could not take her for a wife until he had married Nora. And that could not happen until the lobola was paid in full. The flow of gifts dried up as John started putting aside his savings.

This caused the new girl friend to enter a jealous rage. Together with an accomplice, she went to where John was sleeping off too much native beer. They picked him up and threw him to his death, several floors below. Now no one would be the recipient of John's money, gifts or attention. That's the destructive nature of the "works of the flesh."

Witch Doctor

Leviticus 19:31: "Do not turn to mediums or wizards; do not seek them out, to be defiled by them: I am the LORD your God."

We had been out for the evening and returned to find Nora in tears. Her husband John was dead. I took her to the police station and then to John's brothers where the course of events was learned. John's brothers knew who had committed the crime but had not told the police. We returned home.

The next afternoon, a visitor came to the house looking for Nora. They had an animated conversation. We were later able to learn its content. The visitor was the accomplice. The girl friend had gone to the witch doctor and had a spell put on John's wives in Zululand. Unless everyone agreed not to tell anything to the police, the women would die. Nora, we said, you are an intelligent woman. You don't believe that, do you? She simply shrugged.

About three days letter, a letter for Nora arrived from John's mother in Zululand. John's wives had both been taken violently ill. John's mother had taken them by bull-cart to the mission station. The doctor was puzzled by their ailments, but was certain it was fatal. She had a letter writer pen this note. Please tell John. She had not been told yet about John's death. The time of the onset of the sickness coincided with the time of the visit to the witch doctor.

That evening Nora took the letter to John's brothers. All agreed to be silent. This was communicated to the accomplice, who told the girl friend. She, in turn, went to the witch doctor and had the spell removed. Three days later, another letter arrived. A miracle had occurred. The women were suddenly well. John's mother had walked to the mission station to convey the good news. She still did not know the tragic events in Jo'-burg. Again, the times coincided.

I can't explain this. All I know is that there are forces and powers in this world of which we are unaware. Our hope is to be protected by the power of God.

Obvious?

John 15:9: What do you know that we do not know? What do you understand that is not clear to us?

Our daughter, Marguerite, is an African-American. Her brother, John, is an Asian-American. Both of their parents are white. John was born near the end of spring. Marguerite was born on the first day of winter. Yet their birthdays are only eighteen days apart. Sound almost as obvious as many theological statements?

Rhinoceroses

Isaiah 6:9: And he said, "Go, and say to this people: 'Hear and hear, but do not understand; see and see, but do not perceive.' "

A friend and I went on a photographic safari in the Hluhluwe Game Preserve. This and the neighboring Umfolozi Preserve are set in southeastern South Africa for the protection of white rhinoceroses. Together with a Park Ranger, we walked several miles to our campsite on the site on the banks of the Black Umfolozi River. That night baboons barked at us from the rock face on the opposite bank while hyenas and lions serenaded us with their night noises.

The next couple of days, we looked for rhinos. The parks have two varieties. The white rhino is the larger, weighs two to three tons, with a square face and keen eyesight. The black rhino is about half the white's size, a pointed face and poor vision. The latter is far more dangerous. When we were done taking pictures of the white, the Ranger would yell and wave his hat. The rhinos would lumber off like cattle. It was a different story with the black rhinos. Because everything is blurry, they assume each object is a potential enemy and charge. They are much like us humans who get defensive and attack before we fully view a situation.

A Baboon

Proverbs 22:15: Folly is bound up in the heart of a child, but the rod of discipline drives it far from him.

We were driving through the Kruger Park when we came upon a troop of baboons sitting in the middle of the road. I eased the car to a halt some fifteen feet from them. All of the baboons rushed to the side of the road, except for one little guy who just sat there.

Mother, from her place in safety, scolded him to no avail. Finally deciding we were going to wait, she went to her offspring, picked him up by the scruff of the neck, and carried him to where the other baboons waited. She then turned him over her knee and spanked his behind. His cries indicated that the discipline hurt, but maybe it helped to keep him out of danger. No matter what the source or how painful, we all need discipline.

Give

Matthew 5:42: Give to him who begs from you, and do not refuse him who would borrow from you.

Unwise people often feed wild animals, causing them to learn to beg. In one game preserve, a mother warthog with two young approached the vehicle ahead of us and started begging. Nothing was given. The warthog then circled the car, scrapping a line of paint from it with her tusks.

Jesus' admonitions to give were more for us than the recipient. While they might be assisted by what we offer, it is always in our best interests spiritually to be generous. When we teach them to beg, we both lose.

Tea Party

John 15:19: If you were of the world, the world would love its own; but because you are not of the world, but I chose you out of the world, therefore the world hates you.

Scattered through Kruger Park are rest areas enclosed by high fences. It is only in these that you may get out of your car. Outside the fence the animals roam freely. Inside, you are protected. We were stretching our legs in one of these when a car pulled in.

An obviously British elderly couple got out. They were dressed more for a semi-formal dinner than a game park. He opened their trunk. A wooden chest contained china tea service, crystal goblets, and other finery. They set up a table and chairs, covered the table with a linen cloth, and proceeded to have tea. They were living in a different world. If we as Christians are to be in the world but not of the world, perhaps it could be said we are to have a party in the midst of the wild beasts.

Call

Mark 1:12: The Spirit immediately drove him out into the wilderness. 13: And he was in the wilderness forty days, tempted by Satan;

The Synoptic Gospels relate Jesus struggling with ministry options, three tempting alternatives, and the one he chose. His experience came home when I went through something similar. In rapid succession, a former colleague offered me a research position doing asteroid studies at Kitt Peak Observatory, Smithsonian countered with a choice of several excellent positions, Hughes Aircraft offered a doctoral fellowship for finding their lost satellite and saving them months and millions, and I was accepted into the M. Div. program at Garrett Theological Seminary. My "forty days in the wilderness" was agonizing almost to the point of illness.

God pointed to the answer when a unfamiliar passage of Scripture would not leave me alone. "No one who puts his hand to the plow and looks back is fit for the kingdom of God " (Luke 9:62). When I accepted the ministry I was overwhelmed with a peace and assurance that has never left me. God allows tests to come to clarify and strengthen. But God also shows us the right answer.

Mutti

Numbers 6:24: The LORD bless you and keep you.

A large group of people assembled at the airport to see us off. There were co-workers from the tracking station, some church folks, and Nora. Just before boarding the plane, Nora confessed to us that she had gone to the witch doctor and chewed some mutti, a mixture of herbs prepared for each special purpose. It would ensure that we would have a safe trip and good weather.

Our trip was wonderful and we had no problems. Although we traveled for several weeks through Asia during the rainy season, we had one day of rain. That was on our last day in Japan. Was it the mutti, good fortune, or was it God's way of smiling on us?

New Mexico

Psalm 65:9: Thou visitest the earth and waterest it, thou greatly enrichest it; the river of God is full of water; thou providest their grain, for so thou hast prepared it.

The tracking station was near Las Cruces, New Mexico, and the White Sands. From the green of southern Africa, the arid climate was quite a change. Our landlady had come from Michigan about twenty years before and missed the trees. She had planted an oak in her front yard and watered it with a garden hose each morning.

One day following an unusual rain the night before, we went down and watched the "mighty" Rio Grande River run for the only time during our stay. By late afternoon, the stream was replaced by drying mud.

Earthly blessings are much like that. They come quickly, flow through our lives for a short time, and dry up just as suddenly. The Book of Revelation speaks of a "river of the water of life . . . flowing from the throne of God and of the Lamb" When we tap into God's blessings, we discover that they never run out or dry up.

Jesus Is Lord

Romans 10:9: because, if you confess with your lips that Jesus is Lord and believe in your heart that God raised him from the dead, you will be saved.

Ours was the first class at Garrett Theological Seminary under the new Master of Divinity program. Not content with a simple name change, a comprehensive examination on everything studied was required. I had two fears. First, I do not do well on oral examinations. I mull rather than think quickly. The second had to do with my theology and Christology. Much of mine was based on my reading of the Scriptures without the "benefit" of interpretations through sermons. I prayed diligently that they would not question me on my beliefs as to the Lordship of Jesus.

In preparation, I studied with another student. I was convinced that he had a better grasp of the material than I did. His testing was in the hour before mine. When he told me that he had failed, my heart sank.

After our introduction chat, the first question came at me. "Bob, what do you mean when you say Jesus is Lord?" *I've had it,* I thought. I began my answer. Soon we were in a four-way conversation as to what that expression did and did not mean. With the hour almost gone, I was quickly asked two other (and very easy) questions. I had passed. Once again God had taken a fear and turned it into a blessing.

Question

James 4:11: Do not speak evil against one another, brethren.

We were prepared to go into the mission field. A member of a conservative, independent church approached me with the question, "Are you going to the Philippines to convert the Catholics to Christianity?" I wonder who of us most needs conversion.

Missionary Orientation

I John 4:1: Beloved, do not believe every spirit, but test the spirits to see whether they are of God; for many false prophets have gone out into the world.

Following my graduation from seminary and ordination as Elder, we made our way to Stony Point, New York, and to the interdenominational Missionary Orientation Center. We were to spend six months there learning many things that would eventually be helpful on the mission field, such as techniques for learning a foreign language, sensitivity to other cultures, and the like.

One day was spent in self-inspection as to our motives for being a missionary. Many of our colleagues were angered at the prospect. "I've been called by God," they protested. "That is the reason and the only reason." Throughout the day the leader used a variety of modes in helping us to discovered each had several motivating factors, such as adventure, excitement in living in exotic lands, escape from unpleasant situations, feelings of racial, cultural, or religious superiority, and that it is easier to evangelize among strangers than friends.

All of us discovered that we were acting on a combination of forces within us. It is true for everyone. Not every spirit within us is of God. Therefore, we must continually test the spirits.

Touch

Matthew 8:3: And he stretched out his hand and touched him, saying, "I will; be clean." And immediately his leprosy was cleansed.

Our home in Manila was a mission house behind Philippine Christian College. We had just arrived when our new bishop, Cornelio Ferrer, came by. I invited him in and offered my hand. He took it and held it. For almost an hour, we stood there holding hands as we talked. Initially, I felt uncomfortable. I had been taught that American men don't do something like that. When I realized that it was both good and natural, I relaxed.

On reflection, I remembered that most of Jesus' healings involved touching and, also, that babies often died when deprived of touch. I suspect that we would all be healthier, especially American men, if we were less afraid and reluctant to touch one another.

Impartiality

Acts 10:28: and Peter said to them, "You yourselves know how unlawful it is for a Jew to associate with or to visit any one of another nation; but God has shown me that I should not call any man common or unclean."

Our first task was to get John and Marguerite into schooling. Because we had arrived in mid-January and close to the end of the school year, most schools did not want to admit them. We learned of Faith Academy, a school for the children of conservative, white missionaries from North America. Although I disagree with some of their principles, I am glad they took our children in.

The next term they enrolled in International School, which had a diverse student body. There were nine boys in John's Cub Scout Den. Only two (twin brothers from Vietnam) were from the same country. Isn't it surprising to find more impartiality in a secular group than in a Christian one?

Cebuano

Psalm 137:4: How shall we sing the Lord's song in a foreign land?

Carole and I began our study of Cebuano at the Interchurch Language School in Quezon City. Cebuano is one of over one hundred different languages spoken in the Philippines. My teacher was Ben Aguso. Ben was from Cebu and the master of many languages. I asked Ben where he enjoyed going to church. He said that he worshipped in many churches in many languages. But if he really wanted to worship, he found a church that offered a Cebuano service. Regardless of the quality, that was worship.

Aren't most of us that way? We prefer the style of worship service and hymns with which we grew up. Others may be enlightening or even entertaining, but it is not the "real thing" and we are reluctant to change.

The Spanish

Exodus 34:6: The LORD passed before him, and proclaimed, "The LORD, the LORD, a God merciful and gracious, slow to anger, and abounding in steadfast love . . . but . . . visiting the iniquity of the fathers upon the children and the children's children, to the third and the fourth generation."

In addition to language, we learned about Philippine culture and history. The indigenous people were the Negritos. People from the Malay Archipelago began arriving around 3,000 B.C. Japanese and Chinese traders started visiting about 700 A.D.

In the 13th century, the Mongols swept out of Mongolia. Their invasion of India pushed Islamic peoples into what is Indonesia. From there they spread by the way of Borneo into the southern Philippines by late in the 15th century.

Ferdinand Magellan was both the first known European to visit and the first to die in the Philippines. He was killed by a local chief named Lapu-Lapu on Cebu Island. When Legaspi visited Manila Bay in 1571, he discovered that the local leader was a Muslim named Rajah Suleiman. The Spanish had driven the Muslims out of Spain barely a hundred years earlier and their hatred ran high.

As the Catholic priests won converts to Christianity, they assigned the new believers to fight the "Moros," as the Spanish called them. The resulting hostility continues to this day. The sins of the fathers (Fathers?) are still being passed on.

Independence

Our learning Philippine history necessitated relearning some things we had been taught about the United States. Inspired by Rizal and lead by Aguinaldo and Bonafacio, the Filipinos were in revolt against Spain when the Spanish-American War erupted. Ignited by the sinking of the battleship Maine by parties still unknown, the U.S. formally declared war on Spain on April 25, 1898. The Spanish route of communication to the Philippines was via Spain. On May 1, when Commodore Dewey sailed the American Asiatic Squadron into Manila Bay, the Spanish sailors did not know that a war had been declared. They were standing on deck, saluting their American friends, when Dewey opened fire. All the Spanish ships were sunk with large loss of life. American forces fought alongside Filipino to liberate Manila.

The Philippines declared independence from Spain on June 12, 1898. However, in the peace treaty, which ended the war, Spain ceded the Philippines to the United States. We then declared that the Filipinos were not ready for independence. Prolonged battles ensued, with huge casualties to the Filipino forces. The U.S. finally gave independence to the Philippines on July 4, 1946. Although this date was celebrated for many years, in more recent times, July 4th is Philippine-American Friendship Day. Independence Day is June 12. People are not free when someone else says that they are free but when they think that they are free.

Taal

I Corinthians 12:16: And if the ear should say, "Because I am not an eye, I do not belong to the body," that would not make it any less a part of the body. 17: If the whole body were an eye, where would be the hearing? If the whole body were an ear, where would be the sense of smell?

To celebrate my thirty-fourth birthday, we drove out to Taal Volcano. The active cone sets inside a lake, which is surrounded by the crater of an ancient volcano. We walked down to the lake and took a banca or dug-out canoe to the island. We made our way over the rugged, solidified lava. Ahead of us was the cinder cone. The cinders were like half-inch ball bearings. For every two steps up, we slid back at least one. Finally arriving at the summit, we peered down into the bubbling, steamy volcano.

Once the photographs and sight-seeing was accomplished, it was time to descend. "Kids," I said, "take either my hand or your mother's." Eight-year-old John looked at me and replied, "Yeah, sure, Dad!" And off he ran down the cinder cone. Six-year-old Marguerite was right behind. Then went Carole running down the slope. Needless to say Dad fell six or seven times. John looked at me and said, "Way to go, mountain goat."

I know that I am not an athlete. Neither is an ear an eye. The important thing is to recognize who you are, and then be the best you possibly can.

Bamboo

Ephesians 3:17: (May Christ) dwell in your hearts through faith; that you, being rooted and grounded in love, 18: may have power to comprehend . . . the love of Christ which surpasses knowledge, that you may be filled with all the fullness of God.

The Filipino people have a story about a mango tree that grew near a bamboo. A mango is a large and strong tree, much like a maple or an oak. One day the mango and the bamboo got into an argument as to which was stronger. Both claimed superiority. The mango laughed at the small and swaying bamboo.

Shortly thereafter a hurricane came. The winds blew with great force. The mango stood straight and tall and was soon uprooted by the force of the gale. The bamboo bent with the wind. When the storm was past, the bamboo again stood erect. The mango was destroyed. While we want to be rooted securely so that we are not "tossed to and fro and carried about with every wind of doctrine, by the cunning of men, or by their craftiness in deceitful wiles" (Ephesians 4:14), there are times flexibility is an absolute necessity.

Iligan City

Acts 1:8: But you shall receive power when the Holy Spirit has come upon you; and you shall be my witnesses in Jerusalem and in all Judea and Samaria and to the end of the earth.

Just before Thanksgiving 1969, we left Manila by passenger-carrying freighter for the island of Mindanao. The mission house was located on a large, fenced-in lot, which extended down to Iligan Bay. It was modern, two-storied, and constructed of concrete block. There were several coconut palms, a guava, several flowering trees, and twenty-foot poinsettias.

Our new home and the neighboring Missouri Synod Lutheran mission house were sandwiched between lots in which logging companies dumped the timber for shipment overseas. A quarter mile down the beach was the Iligan Integrated Steel Mill. Across the highway from the house was Tominobo barrio (village). This was to be our home for almost two years. We were finally to get actively involved. After all it is the task of all Christians of being Christ's witnesses to the end of the earth.

Schooling

II Timothy 4:7: I have fought the good fight, I have finished the race, I have kept the faith.

We had enrolled John and Marguerite in Calvert School, an American-based correspondence study. Carole would teach them each morning and periodically sent in lessons and examinations for review and grading. In the afternoon, they went to a "barrio school." Marguerite learned to read English and Cebuano at the same time. They also received instruction about Philippine history and culture, which otherwise would have been denied them.

One such lesson came during an outdoor activity. John's teacher would often organize foot races. The boys would line up and run. When the race was over, John in true American fashion asked, "Who won?" The teacher replied, "It doesn't matter."

John pressed the point. Finally, the teacher asked, "Did you do your best, John?" "Yes." "Then you won. And if your friend Felix did his best, he won. If you do your best, you win." It's not where you end up with regards to others that counts. What really matters is whether or not you did your best.

Feliciano Bergado

Isaiah 6:8: And I heard the voice of the Lord saying, "Whom shall I send, and who will go for us?" Then I said, "Here am I! Send me."

The pastor with whom I worked most closely was the Rev. Feliciano Bergado, who served the Iligan Methodist Church. Feely is a fine pastor, devout Christian, and good friend. We shared many good experiences together. Like most people whom God puts into my life, I was blessed by him. I recall several conversations around a similar topic, the Methodist appointive system. "If you have a change of appointment," I would ask, "what church would you like to serve?" "Wherever God needs me," would be the reply.

Feely was completely convinced that the bishop and his cabinet were all filled with the Holy Spirit. Any church to which he might be appointed was not their will but God's choice. He was willing to go where God wanted him.

Compared with the politics of the American church, I found it hard at first to comprehend his attitude. When I finally did, I admired him for it. When he sings, "Trust and obey, for there's no other way, to be happy in Jesus but to trust and obey," he means it.

Vinaflor

Matthew 14:29: Jesus said, "Come." So Peter got out of the boat and walked on the water and came to Jesus: 30: but when he saw the wind, he was afraid, and beginning to sink he cried out, "Lord, save me."

Vinaflor Mostrales was small, even for a Filipina. She would have had to stand on some books to reach five feet. An excellent deaconess, she was appointed to the Iligan Methodist Church where she worked with the Rev. Feliciano Bergado.

On one occasion there was a conference in another part of Mindanao to which Vina, Feely, and I were to attend. We took a plane from Iligan to Cotabato, then a bus, and then a jeepney. Because of recent rains, we had to walk the last couple of miles over saturated ground. I was carrying Vina's suitcase as well as my own. I was also sinking knee deep in mud while she remained on the surface. She turned and looked at me with a puzzled expression.

"Pastor," she asked, "why are you sinking and I am not?" "How much do you weigh?" "About 40 kilos (88 pounds)." I replied, "I weigh almost 90 kilos (198 pounds), plus I am carrying our suitcases." "Oh," she said with an innocent smile. Who you are affects how you experience life.

Vilma

Mark 5:16: And those who had seen it told what had happened to the demoniac and to the swine, 17: And they began to beg Jesus to depart from their neighborhood.

Vilma was twelve years old and lived in a barrio (small village) on the northern coast of Mindanao. Like most Filipinos, she was Roman Catholic and attended worship regularly. Vilma had the gift of healing. Not that she claimed that she could heal people. She would place her hands on someone, pray to God, and the power would just seem to flow through her.

This went on almost unnoticed until one day she healed the broken leg of a nephew of a bishop. The bishop publicly praised the miracle, and people began flocking to her barrio. A small city of huts quickly grew. There were hundreds of documented healings—broken bones, cancers, TB, etc. Although she only had the strength to heal a few people each day, scores of people would ignore their own physicians and go and wait, with the hope that Vilma would touch and pray for them. Local physicians, suffering a loss of income, sought and received a court injunction banning Vilma from healing. They charged her with practicing medicine without a license. Vilma obeyed and ceased healing.

It seems there are often those who will object to God's miracles, especially if it affects them economically.

The Discipline

Matthew 5:43: "You have heard that it was said, 'You shall love your neighbor and hate your enemy.' 44: But I say to you, Love your enemies and pray for those who persecute you.

The book of rules for The United Methodist Church is called The Discipline. If a Filipino Methodist agrees with what it says, he will quote the relevant passage. When it is contrary, he says, "Oh, that is for the American church. It doesn't apply here." Is that so different from when we say, "The Bible says such-and-such, but that is for the first century Middle Eastern Christians. It doesn't apply to us."

Rotary Club

Psalm 133:1: Behold how good and pleasant it is when brothers dwell in unity!

The Rotary Club in Iligan City was a group of amiable business and professional people. There were Romans Catholics, Protestants, Muslims, Buddhists, and a Sikh. It is sad that such diverse people can get together in social and business settings but not in the area of religion where love and respect should be the rule.

Henry

Matthew 6:19: "Do not lay up for yourselves treasures on earth, where moth and rust consume and where thieves break in and steal, 20: but lay up for yourselves treasures in heaven. . . ."

Henry is an MD, the son of a Methodist pastor. He and his wife Betty met when she was an American Methodist missionary assigned to a rural mobile clinic at which he was the doctor. He could have had a "successful" practice in the United States or in an affluent area of the Philippines. But they chose to make their home in Iligan City, where he set up practice. It is not unusual for him to be paid a chicken or a basket of vegetables for an office visit. He is loved, respected, and at peace with God.

In the eyes of the world, he is not successful. But God doesn't call us to be successful, only faithful.

Floating

Acts 28:26: 'Go to this people, and say, You shall indeed hear but never understands, and you shall indeed see but never perceive."

One of my regular visits was to the church in Santa Cruz barrio of Plaridel. As usual, it took about five hours to reach my destination. I was hot, dusty, and tired. It was Friday afternoon and nothing pressing for me to do. So I went directly to the Pague home where I stayed, changed into my bathing suit, and headed for the water. Iligan Bay was warm and calm. I swam for a bit, then turned over on my back and floated. The sky was a beautiful blue contrasting with the fluffy white clouds. When some time had passed, I had the sensation that I was being watched. A group of a dozen or so persons were gazing in my direction. Standing up in the shallow water, I asked what was the matter. Mr. Bergado, Feliciano's father, spoke up. He had been a fisherman for many years. What I was doing was impossible. "Wood floats, people sink."

The next morning I found the pastor and told him what had transpired. I offered to teach him to float. Soon, the two of us were floating in the sunshine. Again, the crowd gathered. The pastor tried to explain. He got the same reply that I had the day before. "Wood floats, people sink." Seeing is not always believing. How often do you and I see a wonderful thing of God and fail to perceive?

Dapitan

Luke 10:3: But a Samaritan, as he journeyed, came to where he was; and when he saw him, he had compassion.

The congregation at Santa Cruz barrio, Plaridel, had planned an outreach to Dapitan the next time I visited. Therefore, I arrived earlier than usual and we set off for the one-and-a-half-hour drive. There was the pastor, two girls from the Methodist Youth Fellowship, a generator, a 16-mm movie projector, a couple of films, and myself in our Toyota Land Cruiser. Shortly before our destination, we had to detour through a river. The bridge had been washed out. Logging trucks were badly cutting up the make-shift road.

After supper we set up on the beach. With dusk we started the films and soon had a crowd. The pastor read Scripture, preached, and prayed. The girls sang. The response of the people was encouraging. When the service was over, we left with high spirits for the return trip. The temporary road at the detour had been impassable. I took a chance on the other side of the bridge. We went down the hill, through the river, zigzagged between the coconut trees, and up the other side. I paused to shift it out of four-wheel drive.

As we started one of the girls said, "There are some people there!" Three college men and a coed had been on a bus. The driver had stopped and told them to cross over the foot bridge. There would be a bus waiting. They did. No bus. They all crowded in with us. Again, I started to go.

"What about them?" asked one of the students. A woman with four kids and two big sacks of rice were also sitting in the dark. The three male students rode in back with the rice, generator, and projector. The woman and four kids joined the girls in the back seat. The coed sat between the pastor and myself. As we inched down the road, the low beams of the headlight shown on the tops of the trees. After about a half hour, the woman said, "This is where I live." We unloaded her, her kids and rice. She promised she would have a Mass said for me the next day. I thanked her.

A few minutes later, we had passed through a barrio, a single 60-watt bulb hanging from a post. A couple of hundred yards farther on, a man lay in the middle of the road. Illuminating him with the headlights, I was about to get out. "He might be hurt," the pastor objected. "Yes," I said. "He might be dead." "Yes."

I got out as did one of the college men. There was no sign of injury. He was breathing and had a strong pulse. Suddenly, a light shone from twenty or so yards off the road. A woman appeared silhouetted in a doorway. "What's happening?" she asked. "There's a man in the road," I answered. "My husband," she screamed. They had had a fight and he had gone into the barrio. After too much coconut wine, he passed out before reaching home. We picked him up and carried him in. He was limp. The entire distance his wife called him things, which I refuse to translate, but told of the shame he had brought by having a Cano (Americano) help him home.

As we began driving again, my passengers began talking. The voices grew animated, but hushed. Curious, I strained to hear what was being said. "Just like the Good Samaritan." Apparently I had just preached the best sermon of my life without saying a word and without knowing it. It made me realize that people are watching as we live out our faith.

Translation

Matthew 7:15: "Beware of false prophets, who come to you in sheep's clothing but inwardly are ravenous wolves."

Bishop and Mrs. Ferrer wanted to visit the churches of northern Mindanao. I was the designated driver. One stop took us to Santa Cruz barrio, Plaridel. We arrived early afternoon and spread the word that the bishop would be speaking that evening. The church was filled. Bishop Ferrer spoke several languages but Cebuano, which was spoken locally, was not one of them. The pastor of the church served as translator.

That night I heard two very different messages. The one in English by the bishop. The other in Cebuano by the pastor. The latter wanted to "improve" on the words of the former. Since then I have had my suspicions of translations whether they are of speeches, documents, or even the Scriptures. Subconsciously or deliberately, many translators seek to "improve" on that which was provided. Jesus' words provide warning. "Beware!"

Darkness

John 12:35: Jesus said to them, "The light is with you for a little longer. Walk while you have the light, lest the darkness overtake you; he who walks in the darkness does not know where he goes."

The bus taking me to Plaridel arrived after dark. It was a couple of miles to Santa Cruz barrio, but I knew the way well. Having been an astronomer, I knew that there is always sky brightness. Once your eyes are acclimatized, you can see adequately well.

It turned out to be the blackest night I have ever experienced. I eased my way along by feel.

The gravel told me I was on the road. A couple of times, I almost stumbled. When I felt wood beneath my feet, I knew that I was on the bridge crossing the river. After inching along for about an hour, I caught the faint glimmer of a light in the barrio. The pleasure at seeing the light was a dim reminder of the great joy of encountering The Light.

Stationary

Psalm 46:10: "Be still, and know that I am God. I am exalted among the nations, I am exalted in the earth!"

I often traveled by bus in the Philippines and quickly learned that there were three classes of service. The "Local" stopped at any town, barrio, house, or wide place in the road. The "Express" would stop only in villages and designated points. The fastest and most efficient class or service was the "Stationary," which stopped only at the stations.

The terms remind me of many of us Christians. We jump into the express lane when God wants us stationary. And when God tells us to go, we opt for the stationary mode.

Malaybalay

Isaiah 43:19: Behold, I am doing a new thing; now it springs forth, do you not perceive it? I will make a way in the wilderness and rivers in the desert.

It was a couple of hours drive eastward along the northern coast of Mindanao to Cagayan de Oro, a modest-sized city with a busy port and large Delmonte pineapple processing facility. Turning south, it was another two-hour drive on winding roads through the mountains to reach Malaybalay.

The small Methodist congregation there struggled to support their pastor. He and his family had been housed in two small rooms at the rear of the church. With the assistance of the men of the district in a work project, a two-story concrete building was constructed. The upper level provided a home for the pastor. The lower one was rented as a drug store with that income supplementing the pastor's salary. It was a new and creative approach to their problems. It is easy to forget that we are made in the image of the God who does new things.

Multi-Purpose Buildings

Matthew 25:21: His master said to him, 'Well done, good and faithful servant; you have been faithful over a little, I will set you over much; enter into the joy of your master.'

Although the Malaybalay parsonage was unique, multi-purpose buildings were not unusual. Private schools would use the same building extensively. In the morning it was filled with grade school children. In the afternoon, high school students were there. They were replaced by the college classes in the evening.

The Roman Catholic Church leads the way as far as multi-purpose buildings for worship. Often in a barrio instead of erecting a traditional church they would build essentially a pole-building without walls and with a concrete-slab floor. On Sunday morning the priest would remove what he needed for the Mass from a nearby shed and replace it following the service. Then the basketball backboards would be lowered, and it was used for recreation. During the daylight hours on weekdays, it was used for drying grain or similar purposes. In the evenings it housed classes or recreation or dances.

If we contrast this with our multi-million dollar buildings, which are used for a few hours each week, to whom do you think the Lord would say, "Well done, good and faithful servant, you have been faithful over a little. . . ."

Kaingin

Psalm 107:33: He turns rivers into a desert, springs of water into thirsty ground, 34: a fruitful land into a salty waste, because of the wickedness of its inhabitants.

In the mountain areas, the reverse effect of reforestation could be seen. Many of the loggers were conscientious and had cut only the big trees, leaving the smaller ones to hold the soil and reforest the hillsides. However they are often followed by the "kaingin," slash-and-burn farmers. The latter would clear cut a couple of acres and plant crops—papaya, sugar cane, corn, vegetables. Within a couple of years, the rains will have washed the top soil down into the valleys and the fertility of the land is gone. The farmer moves on to despoil another piece of ground.

As a result of their activity, the climate on Mindanao is also changing. Typhoons now occur where they once were absent.

Flooding is common following rains. Formerly the climate was almost uniform year around. Now it is becoming marked by distinctive seasons of hot and cold, rain and dry. I'm not sure if God is doing it because of the wickedness of the inhabitants or if they are doing it to themselves. Maybe there isn't much difference.

Land

Genesis 13:14: The LORD said to Abram . . . "Lift up your eyes, and look from the place where you are, northward and southward and eastward and westward; 15: for all the land which you see I will give to you and to your descendants forever."

Who owns the land? The Filipinos who have been influenced by the Spanish and the Americans assume that it is the person who holds the deed owns the land. The tribal people, much like the Native Americans, assume that no one owns the land. It is just there. If it is unused it is available. Conflicts are frequent. "Squatter, get off my land." "It's everyone's land. You weren't using it, so I did." If judged by their basic assumptions each one is right, but they are sharply different. Like most cultural and religious squabbles, it is a matter not of truths but of assumptions.

Jokes

John 14:9: Jesus said to him, "Have I been with you so long, and yet you do not know me, Philip?"

I was one of the leaders at the annual Methodist Youth Fellowship's Christmas Institute. During a break in activities, several of the leaders began telling jokes. Each of my Philippine colleagues told a story and everyone except myself laughed. I didn't get it. Then it was my turn. They didn't understand. To grasp a joke, a parable, or even an issue of faith, one has to be immersed in the culture. Otherwise you just don't get it.

Deaconesses

Galatians 3:28: There is neither Jew nor Greek, there is neither slave nor free, there is neither male nor female; for you are all one in Christ Jesus.

The Methodist Church in the Philippines has an extensive and excellent deaconesses program. These well-trained and talented women serve the church in a variety of ways. When a congregation is given the choice between having a pastor or a deaconess, they generally opt for the latter. A pastor, they claim, can only visit and preach. A deaconess can do both of those. Plus she can play the piano, teach kindergarten and other classes, work with the women, . . . It is not the title or the gender that is important, but how well you serve the Lord.

Most Beautiful Woman

Psalm 59:8: But thou, O LORD, dost laugh at them; thou dost hold all the nations in derision.

To reach the Cebu church, I had to travel by plane or overnight deck passage by ship. I usually chose the latter. There were several ships that plied the waters between Mindanao and Cebu. The most popular was the Mv. Fatima. The Catholics liked it because of her name. It reminded them of the incident at Fatima, Portugal, where three young girls saw successive visions of the Virgin Mary, the most beautiful woman in the world.

The Muslims liked the ship because of its name also. Both the ship and that village in Portugal were named for the daughter of the prophet Muhammad, Fatima, the most beautiful woman in the world. I don't know about "laughter" or the "derision," but I am quite sure the good Lord at least chuckled.

Cebu

Luke 12:18: And he (the fool) said, 'I will do this: I will pull down my barns, and build larger ones; and there I will store all my grain and my goods."

The United Church of Christ in the Philippines' Cebu congregation had a thriving membership in a building far too small for their needs. Having sufficient property they constructed a large, modern church behind the old one. Before they could tear down the old building, many people objected. It was all right to build and worship in the new building, but there were too many memories to demolish the old. They still walk around the empty old church to reach the new. The fool in the parable tore down the old to build new. The church built new and could not tear down the old. What Jesus would say?

Spirits

Matthew 8:16: That evening they brought to him many who were possessed with demons; and he cast out the spirits with a word, and healed all who were sick.

Belief in spirits is widespread. There are witches and ghouls and vampires. There are also spirits that inhabit trees, rocks, and bushes. Certain types of vegetation are not cut for fear of spirits. Night pots are used by the entire family, but just emptied anyplace in the morning. When asked why not go out to relieve oneself, the usual answer is, "What if you urinate on an unseen spirit in the dark?" The results could be devastating. Some of these beliefs are helpful and would be like warning children to avoid angering the spirit of the poison ivy vine.

But beliefs in spirits also harmfully keeps people from positive actions out of fear. We call them neuroses and phobias. Regardless of the name, if it keeps us from abundant living and fulfilling God's purpose for our lives, it needs to be cast out.

Three Gods?

Deuteronomy 6:4: "Hear, O Israel: The LORD our God is one LORD."

A Filipino friend is a Jehovah's Witness. In one of our congenial talks about faith, he claimed that most Philippine Christians believe in three gods. I assured him that he must be mistaken. Perhaps he didn't understand the concept of the Trinity. I proceeded to explain to him how the early Church used the masks in the Greek plays to describe the Trinity. The masks, called "personna" in Greek, were used to reveal which character an actor was portraying. The Church said that God used three masks to reveal himself to us. One God in three "personna"—God's revealing role of loving Creator; God's revealing presence in Jesus the Christ, and God's revealing work in you and me. Unfortunately in English, "personna" becomes "person." One God, in three persons, often implies three personalities. He said that he understood that, but that I should listen carefully.

The following Sunday, I was sitting in a Sunday School class. The discussion was on the first chapter of Genesis. When we came to the 26th verse ("Then God said, 'Let us make man in our image, after our likeness,' . . ."), the consensus was that God the Father called a consultation. He checked it out with God the Son and God the Holy Spirit. They all agreed to the proposed action.

But what, I asked, about God being one? It was politely explained to me that it was like a marriage. When a man and a woman agree in wedlock, they become one. So it is with God, they said. When the three Gods agree on a single purpose, they are One. I was upset. I wondered if it bothered God.

Jehovah's Witnesses

Matthew 28:19: Go therefore and make disciples of all nations, baptizing them in the name of the Father and of the Son and of the Holy Spirit.

Primed more by rumor than by knowledge, the local clergy got visibly upset with the arrival of the Jehovah's Witnesses. The Witnesses had to be anti-Christian because they rejected the doctrine of the Trinity. Playing on those fears and knowing the basis of that doctrine, the Jehovah's Witnesses would challenge the clergy to a public debate. The clergy welcomed the opportunity to discredit these enemies of the faith.

As the debate began, the Witnesses would suggest some rules. Primarily that all arguments be based solely on Scripture. That sounded reasonable. The Witnesses would then easily win the debate. By agreeing on the Scripture-only condition, the clergy had lost almost all of their ammunition. The verse from Matthew, which is cited above, is the only reference to the Trinity in the entire Bible. Most Scripture verses favor the Witnesses' position.

The early Church in presenting the doctrine of the Trinity did so, not from Scripture, but from experience. They had experienced God's revealing love in God's creativity, in God's presence in Jesus, and in God's inner dwelling in us. So despite their efforts, the clergy failed in their goal. Enthusiasm is seldom the equal of wisdom, nor is knowledge on a par with experience.

All Saints' Day

Luke 4:8: And Jesus answered him, "It is written, 'You shall worship the Lord your God, and him only shall you serve.' "

After Good Friday, All Saints' Day is the next most important religious day in the Philippines. Tombs are white-washed and decorated. Candlelight vigils are kept throughout All Saints' Eve night. Many communities hold religious parades and processions. Ceremonies are observed in churches and in cemeteries.

One All Saints' Day, we were visiting a large cemetery. In the Chinese section, plates of prepared food sat on the tombs so that the deceased might enjoy the "spiritual essence" of their favorite dishes.

One man was burning what appeared to be play money. He informed us that it was "spirit money," which he had purchased at the Chinese temple. Burning, he said, transformed it from the physical to the spiritual realm in order that his parents might have money to spend in the spirit world. He quickly added that he was a Christian and didn't believe in it. But since his parents did, he was honoring them. On All Saints Day he had combined a Christian celebration with that of pagan ancestor worship.

Haven't we done much the same? We mingle celebrating Jesus' resurrection with the spring devotion of Ishtar (also called Astarte and Easter), goddess of fertility, with her symbols of bunnies, chicks, ducks and eggs. Sometimes it is difficult to keep our worship pure from containmants.

Chinese

I Corinthians 7:9: But if they cannot exercise self-control, they should marry. For it is better to marry than to be aflame with passion.

Many of the Philippine laws are blatantly anti-Chinese. It is virtually impossible for a Chinese individual to become a Philippine citizen. Despite this the Chinese have found a way to make the laws work for them. Suppose a Chinese man goes to the Philippines where he meets and falls in love with a Filipina. They will get married in the church and "in the sight of God" but omit the legalities. Since they are not legally married, the children are hers and are Philippine citizens. Later, they go to city hall for the legal ceremony. Now any children born are his and would be Chinese citizens. If they are merchants, you would have brothers, some of whom are citizens of the Philippines and others of China involved in the export/import business.

Should we do something similar for senior citizens? Suppose that her late husband had worked and earned a fair pension. She worked hard at home while raising the families so that he could devote his energies to his job. If she remarries, she loses his pension. He is a widower with grown children and an adequate pension. Together with both pensions and Social Security, they can have a modest income. Life would be difficult if they lost any portion of it. His children are adamantly opposed to his remarriage for fear of losing an inheritance. If they live together without marriage, although they have companionship and love, they feel guilty and sinful. If they get legally married, they lose income and relationship with families. How would love respond?

Motives

Matthew 24:14: And this gospel of the kingdom will be preached throughout the whole world, as a testimony to all nations; and then the end will come.

We had American friends who were with a group translating the Gospels into languages for which there were no Scripture portions available. We admired their efforts. It was difficult and time-consuming work. However, their motivation was bothersome. This couple apparently had no love or regard for the people with whom they labored. Instead, they took the above text literally and saw their task as simply hastening Christ's return. Where other people were in terms of a judgment was not their concern. They "knew" that they were okay. Thankfully, as illustrated by the story of Jonah, God can use our efforts even if our hearts are not in it.

Lonely

Psalm 25:16: Turn thou to me, and be gracious to me; for I am lonely and afflicted. 17: Relieve the troubles of my heart, and bring me out of my distresses.

Another missionary had been the auxiliary chaplain at the U.S. Air Force Weather Station, just south of Cagayan de Oro. He was returning to the States. Would I take over? There were thirty men at the station including six officers. I spent one or two Monday nights each month there. They didn't want religious services or in-depth counseling. The need was for someone to talk to. That and "Chaplain, will you watch a movie with me?" By the time the film was over, another man had drifted in. As the first man departed, the second would raise the same question. One night I watched five full-length movies.

Despite our over-crowded world, many of God's people are lonely and crying out for someone to listen and share.

Salt

Matthew 5:13: "You are the salt of the earth; but if salt has lost its taste, how shall its saltness be restored?"

Scattered along the coast are villages where the primary source of income is from fishing. Since refrigeration is still a rare commodity in many places, the fish and shrimp are spread out in the sun on woven mats, periodically sprinkled with sea water and dried. The products will keep for months. Without the salt from the sea water, the fish would just rot. The salt preserves it.

Many suggestions have been made regarding Jesus statement, "You are the salt of the earth." We as salt enhance the flavor, make people thirsty for the Living Water, and act as an antiseptic. Perhaps. But we are also to preserve those who would otherwise rot and stink like dead fish.

Literacy

Matthew 25:40: And the King will answer them, "Truly, I say to you, as you did it to one of the least of these my brethren, you did it to me."

Dansalan College in Marawi City continues founder Frank Laubach's literacy outreach. Persons are taught to read, write, and do simple arithmetic. After they have developed their skills, they receive a monthly publication containing items on current events, health, religion, and other matters that affect the well-being of the community.

I attended a graduation for about two dozen persons, including two barrio mayors. As part of the ceremony, participants demonstrated their skills. One mayor read haltingly, but was cheered by the audience. The other mayor struggled with a math problem. He too was applauded. They all were proud. The teaching had been done for "the least of these." I think Jesus was smiling as he received his diploma.

Feeding the Hungry

Matthew 25:34: Then the King will say to those at his right hand, "Come, O blessed of my Father, inherit the kingdom prepared for you from the foundation of the world; 35: for I was hungry and you gave me food."

Most of the people in and near Marawi City are poor and malnourished. Two of Dansalan College programs were addressed to those needs. There was an agricultural project that had three equally important foci. First, find out what would grow well in that environment. Second, it had to be high in nutrition. Third, the people had to be willing to eat it!

There was also a weaving project. If the women could make salable products, the family income would increase and poverty would decrease. Japanese looms were introduced to replace the inefficient back-looms. The women were to make products which could be sold worldwide. This included the necessity to make many exact duplicates of the item for things like place mats.

105

There is an old saying that if a person is hungry and you give him a fish, he will be hungry again. But if you teach him to fish, he will never be hungry. In Christ's name, Dansalan College was "teaching the people to fish." Isn't that part of all of our jobs as Christians?

The Clinic

Luke 10:8: Whenever you enter a town and they receive you, eat what is set before you; 9: heal the sick in it and say to them, "The kingdom of God has come near to you."

On campus was The Clinic, which specialized in maternal and child health. A Muslim woman is not allowed to be seen unclothed by any male other than her husband. Unless her husband is a doctor, she had better remain healthy. The Clinic employed two Christian women doctors and several female midwives. The response to the service was at times overwhelming. Because infant mortality was so high, some mothers boarded their babies at the clinic for up to a year to ensure their survival.

Every year there was a Well Baby Clinic. Mothers of children born in the clinic were urged to bring their children back. The youngsters were examined. At the end of the day, prizes of vitamins, powered milk, or some other health-inducing items were given out. Everyone received a prize. Every child had an annual check-up.

We who have access to good health care and often take it for granted should look around and continually thank God.

Familiar

II Corinthians 1:3: Blessed be the . . . God of all comfort, 4: who comforts us in all our affliction, so that we may be able to comfort those who are in any affliction . . .

Women needing to stay in the clinic for treatment were often accompanied by their family. As in earlier days in our country, the notion was held that a hospital is where you go to die. The presence of family made it less scary. The family also cooked the food for the patient. Because it was home-style cooking, the patient responded better than to strange institutional food.

In clinics or in churches when we provide the familiar to those whom we are trying to serve, they become comfortable. When they are comfortable, they are more ready to accept what we have to offer.

Durian

Psalm 34:8: Oh, taste and see that the LORD is good! Happy is the man who takes refuge in him!

In the southern Philippines is a fruit in the breadfruit family known as the durian. It is about the size of a volleyball and is covered with large spikes. Inside the thick green husk are several large black seeds. Each is covered with white sweet delicious meat. The problem is the aroma. Eating durian has been compared to eating strawberries and cream in a badly-kept outhouse. Many people have either an instant love or instant dislike for the durian. For others, the taste has to be developed. Isn't it that way with God also.

Zenaida

Matthew 4:1: Then Jesus was led up by the Spirit into the wilderness to be tempted by the devil.

Our student body was comprised of both Christians and Muslims. All students were required to take *The Literature of the Bible* and *The History of Islam.* It was an exciting challenge to teach a mixed group about the others' faith and theirs. We were beginning the New Testament. Since Matthew had written his Gospel for people of a Semitic culture, it is good for both Muslim and Christian students.

After reading several chapters, each person was to write a paper. Zenaida Lomondot was the brightest student in the class. Her choice was "Jesus' Temptation." She wrote that Jesus was able to resist Satan because he had been fasting. When I read it, I said to myself, "Of course. How could I have missed something so obvious?" We in the West seem to believe that if you fast you get weak. The naturalist would tell us that in mankind's early days it was a cycle of kill—eat—lethargy—hunger—alertness—kill. Sages from most religious traditions will tell us that fasting is the route to heighten mental and spiritual powers. It is a source of strength and grace that we too often ignore.

Christ spoke to me through a young Muslim coed. I continually wonder whom God will use next.

Avenger

Matthew 5:38: "You have heard that it was said, 'An eye for an eye and a tooth for a tooth.' 39: But I say to you, Do not resist one who is evil. But if any one strikes you on the right cheek, turn to him the other also."

Somerado was a tall, good-looking young man and one of my college students. He also had permission to carry a loaded .45 caliber automatic pistol to class. It seems that his uncle, a retired army general, was in charge of security for a logging firm.

One day uncle was at a logging camp with his son making an inspection. They spent the night in a tent. It was their custom for the general to sleep on the lower bunk, but that night they switched.

In the middle of the night, someone sprayed the lower part of the tent with bullets. The son was killed. The family investigated and called a meeting. The guilty party was a mayor of a distant barrio. Revenge was needed. Somerado volunteered to protect the family honor. Riding his motorcycle to the barrio, he waited for and killed the mayor. Then he returned home. The mayor's family was outraged. Yes, the mayor was guilty. But the life of a mayor is worth more than the life of a general's son. They wanted equity.

Until a probably monetary settlement could be reached, Somerado carried a weapon. I am distressed over the number of "Christians" who prefer this form of "justice" than that to which Jesus calls us.

Parables

Matthew 13:24: Another parable he put before them, saying, "The kingdom of heaven may be compared to a man who sowed good seed in his field . . ."

One of the challenges of a teacher is to explain that which is beyond the experience of the students. Most of my physics students in both college and high school did not have either electricity or running water in their homes. To bring them to an understanding of modern science, one essentially uses parables. It is like saying "How shall I get this across to you? The flow of electricity is like the nearby Maria Cristina falls. Voltage is like the height of the falls. If there is no height, there is no flow of water. The higher the elevation, the more energy. The current in a wire is like the current in the river. Amperage is a measure of how much water is passing by." And so on.

This is what Jesus is doing with the many parables he tells concerning the kingdom of God. It is almost as if he is saying, "How shall I get this across to you? Let me try this. The kingdom of God may be compared to . . ." It is up to us "students" to grasp what he means.

Elaine's Baptism

Proverbs 22:6: Train up a child in the way he should go, and when he is old he will not depart from it.

Our home in Marawi City was across the road from the campus of Dansalan College. It was two-story, with front porches on both levels, wood frame, built in the late twenties, and badly needing paint. Our "family" lived on the top floor. There was

Carole, John, Marguerite, and myself. In addition, Inday and Myrna were college students who assisted Carole with the housework in exchange for room, board, tuition, and some spending money. Noe, a high school student, had a similar arrangement. Downstairs lived the Espinas. He was a sometimes student. She was a college English teacher.

On Monday evenings we had a Bible study in our living room. Our extended family was joined by the Espinas and eight others from the staff. We had been studying baptism when Mrs. Espina came to me with a request. She was Protestant. He was Catholic. She wanted her two-month old baby Elaine baptized. Could I help?

On a Sunday afternoon a few weeks later, our entire study group went down to Iligan Bay. We grilled fish on an open fire and had a picnic. We swam and played games on the beach. Then we all went into the water and baptized Elaine. John, ten, and Marguerite, eight, both seemed bored with that part of the day.

Almost a decade later, John was married and the father of a son, Jason. His wife, Ginny, and Carole were having a discussion on having Jason baptized. They were talking about the possibilities of a church service when John spoke up. "We will do it like Elaine!" By then we owned some land with a river running through it. We have now baptized six grandchildren in the Black River all because God had spoken to an apparently disinterested youth in a way he couldn't forget.

Woodstock

Matthew 3:16: And when Jesus was baptized, he went up immediately from the water, and behold, the heavens were opened and he saw the Spirit of God descending like a dove, and alighting on him.

We had several pets. There were two dogs, Whitney and Ursula, a cat named Ming, a civet called Rascal, and a pigeon we called Woodstock. The five ate from the same bowl at the same time and got along fine. They each had special characteristics. Woodstock is especially remembered for his habit of landing on your head when you were walking in the yard. So softly was it that often you did not realize his presence. Then you felt his toenails as he turned in circles.

I have problems with symbols of the Holy Spirit that look like a cross between a pelican's power dive for a fish and a bird that has been dropped by a shotgun. The Holy Spirit descends on us like a dove—softly, gently, lovingly.

Sensitivity

Matthew 13:15: For this people's heart has grown dull, and their ears are heavy of hearing, and their eyes they have closed, lest they should perceive with their eyes, and hear with their ears, and understand with their heart, and turn for me to heal them.

Marawi City had a population near 40,000. There was no sewer system or garbage collection. The half dozen septic systems were all on our college campus. The city water was one hydrant, which ran once a week. Everyone had sinus conditions. TB was prevalent. Malnutrition was rampant. Initially we were very aware of our surroundings and appalled by conditions. But it is amazing how quickly one loses that sensitivity. Within a few weeks, we did not "see" the garbage. It was just how things were. Then a visitor would remind us.

There are many people who lose their sensitivity for God's work and presence in the world and are just waiting for us to remind them.

Spiritual Gifts

I Corinthians 12:4: Now there are varieties of gifts, but the same Spirit.

I was representing our college at a science teachers' seminar. A colleague was a very sad young man. He was talented, caring, and had a deep faith. He had recently been removed from leadership in his church because he didn't speak in tongues. I tried my best to affirm his worth and faith. When will we all learn that there are varieties of gifts but that love (which does not insist on its own way) is the greatest and should be our aim?

Colors

Exodus 26:1: "Moreover you shall make the tabernacle with ten curtains of fine twined linen and blue and purple and scarlet stuff; with cherubim skilfully worked shall you make them."

Why "blue and purple and scarlet?" Did those colors mean something? We often assume that there is a universal meaning of colors. Red always means stop and green means go. But that was not always true. I have a railroad switch lamp that was used before standardization and has blue and amber lenses. For most Christians black symbolizes death.

But in the Muslim Philippines, as in much of southeast Asia, white serves that purpose. A house will be draped with white cloth if there has been a recent death, except if it was caused by someone and retribution has not been satisfied. Then it is draped in red cloth. Like so many things in life, there are a variety of interpretations and a mutual understanding is needed.

Muslim Marriage

Genesis 24:37: My master made me swear, saying, "You shall not take a wife for my son from the daughters of the Canaanites, in whose land I dwell; 38: but you shall go to my father's house and to my kindred, and take a wife for my son."

In Muslim society, three persons are required to enact a marriage. It is the groom, the groom's father, and the bride's father. The bride does not have to be present, consent or even know that she is getting married. What we might perceive as injustice is not limited to brides. In my second full year of teaching at Dansalan College, I was requested to teach high school physics as well as in the college. My students were about seventeen years old.

One Tuesday, following class, one of the boys, Ali Mingca, came up to me. "Sir," he said, "I will be absent tomorrow." "Okay," I replied. "Why is that, Ali?" He looked at the floor and said, "My parents told me last night that I'm getting married tomorrow." Trying to be understanding, I said, "Have you met the girl, Ali?" "No, sir" he answered. "But I think I saw her once."

Ali was absent the following day but in class the next. After class I approached him. "Did you get married?" "Yes, sir." "Is she a nice girl" "I think so."

As I look at our lack of success in producing stable marriages, we certainly can't point fingers at arranged ones. The Bible only says that a marriage is "what therefore God has joined together," not how he wants it done.

Divorce

Matthew 19:8: He said to them, "For your hardness of heart Moses allowed you to divorce your wives, but from the beginning it was not so."

The bride price amongst the Maranao Muslims with whom we were living was substantial. It was very unusual for a man to afford it without help. Even if they had to borrow the money, all of his kin folks would contribute. This resulted in a low divorce rate. If the bride left her husband, the bride price would have to be returned. By then it was probably gone to help finance a kinsman's wedding. Likewise, the groom knew that his family contributed to his first marriage. The next would be completely on his own. Although divorce was possible, financial pressures and families kept couples together. That might not be the best reason to stay married, but it works better than our system.

Income Tax

Matthew 10:16: "Behold, I send you out as sheep in the midst of wolves; so be wise as serpents and innocent as doves."

I had paid my Philippine income tax that day. In the evening a visitor came. He introduced himself as the Provincial Treasurer. He had my check and inquired if I could take it back and give him cash. He wasn't required to forward the money to the federal government for several months and wanted to use it in the interim. I knew arguments about impropriety would do no good. "I would like to," I said, "but all those officials in Manila are a bunch of crooks. I need the canceled check as proof that I paid." Nodding his head in agreement, he went off. You have to speak in a language people understand.

House on the Rocks

Matthew 7:24: "Every one then who hears these words of mine and does them will be like a wise man who built his house upon the rock."

The Philippines has several active volcanoes and many ancient ones. It is therefore prone to earthquakes. In Marawi are several houses built upon the rocks. The wooden footings for the house rest upon a dozen or so stones about three feet in diameter.

Jesus could have used this image as well. When the earth moves beneath your feet, your house (of faith) will stand because it is built upon the rocks.

Harem-ette

Job 21:9: Their houses are safe from fear, and no rod of God is upon them.

This unusual house was two-storied with the family dwelling quarters on the upper level. Separated from it by a few feet and resting on a huge post almost ten foot tall was a house of similar design but only about twelve feet square. It had a removal ramp, which connected it to the family area of the main house. This was the abode of the unmarried daughters. When visitors come to the house, the girls went to their apartment and removed the access. I know some American fathers who wish they could do similarly to protect their daughters.

Good Measure

Luke 6:38: "Give, and it will be given to you; good measure, pressed down, shaken together, running over, will be put into your lap. For the measure you give will be the measure you get back."

I was in the market one day, watching people and enjoying the aromas. I paused near a man who was selling rice, flour, sugar, and other bulk commodities. The items were sold by the volume, not by weight, from large open bins. He had a wooden box with the top missing with which he measured. As I watched, a couple came to purchase some brown sugar. The seller used his fingers and proceeded to fluff-up the sugar in the bin, creating air pockets in the sugar. Then he carefully scooped up the sugar into the ganta container, scraped off that which extended above the top of the box, and dumped it into the sack. He repeated this several times.

During the process, he noticed that I was watching. He gave me a sly smile and I nodded my acknowledgment. We both knew that he was cheating the customers. They were receiving about two-thirds of what a well-packed container would hold. How different this is from God, who when we act with love, gives back "good measure, pressed down, shaken together, running over."

Disgrace

Matthew 5:38: "You have heard that it was said, 'An eye for an eye and a tooth for a tooth.' 39: But I say to you, Do not resist one who is evil. But if any one strikes you on the right cheek, turn to him the other also; . . . and do not refuse him who would borrow from you."

One morning, Carole and I were awakened early by a nearby gunshot. Rushing to our front porch, we arrived in time to see our neighbor from across the street being loaded into the sidecar of a motorcycle. His chest was bleeding profusely. A few hours later, his body was returned from the hospital for the burial preparations. We later learned that he had been shot by his cousin, who was also his brother-in-law since they had married sisters.

Some time previously the cousin had loaned our neighbor one hundred pesos (about sixteen dollars U.S.). Several attempts to collect the loan had failed. Meanwhile, the cousin was forced to borrow money from someone outside the family and was being pressed to repay it. He had come that morning to try once more to collect. Our neighbor refused. The cousin was "forced" to shoot our neighbor to keep their family from being disgraced in the community. Instead of losing face, his action caused them to gain respect. They were seen as a people who would go to the extremes to pay their debts to those outside the family. How far would you and I go so that our Christian family would not be disgraced in the community?

Sin versus Shame

John 10:10: The thief comes only to steal and kill and destroy; I came that they may have life, and have it abundantly.

The previous story illustrates an aspect of life in much of East Asia. Guilt relates to an individual and is relatively rare. Shame relates to a community and is very prevalent. While specific items that cause shame vary from culture to culture, anything that an individual does that brings disgrace to one's community is a source of shame for that individual. The unsuccessful Japanese warrior would commit suicide because of his shame.

When Roman Catholic missionaries arrived in the Philippines, they discovered this situation and adjusted their theology appropriately. Sin can result in shame just as well as in guilt. The Protestants didn't know what to do with shame. But they had this wonderful cure for guilt. They proceeded to make the Filipinos guilty so that they could use their medicine. Perhaps they learned it from the advertising folks. If you don't have a need for what we have to offer, we'll create that need. I don't think that is what Jesus had in mind when he offered people abundant life.

Sultan Alonto

Matthew 7:21: "Not every one who says to me, 'Lord, Lord,' shall enter the kingdom of heaven, but he who does the will of my Father who is in heaven."

At a gathering of Muslim and Christian leaders, Sultan Alonto, a local Muslim leader, spoke about his people. "They are not true Muslims," he said. "The Creed is meaningless to them. They do not pray as they should. If they go on pilgrimage, it is for economic or political reasons. They might fast during the day in Ramadan, but they feast all night. They are Muslims in name only."

Apparently it is not only the followers of Jesus who have trouble distinguishing between being acquaintances and being disciples.

Genealogy

Luke 3:23: Jesus, when he began his ministry, was about thirty years of age, being the son (as was supposed) of Joseph, the son of Heli, . . . the son of Judah, 34: the son of Jacob, the son of Isaac, the son of Abraham, . . . the son of Seth, the son of Adam, the son of God.

A prominent Muslim neighbor had died. The funeral was held that day, as was the custom. That night his genealogy was recited over a speaker system so the entire area could hear. Starting with the deceased, his heritage was traced back through his family and shortly before dawn ended with Adam, who was created by God. Whether accurate or not, the process is a good reminder. Ultimately, we must all trace our roots back to God, our creator.

Refugees

James 2:15: If a brother or sister is ill-clad and in lack of daily food, 16: and one of you says to them, "Go in peace, be warmed and filled," without giving them the things needed for the body, what does it profit? 17: So faith by itself, if it has no works, is dead.

The sporadic acts of violence between Christians and Muslims had erupted into attacks on villages. People fled their homes in the middle of the night carrying only a few meager possessions. Almost 15,000 refugees flooded into Marawi City. That meant that about every fourth person on the street was displaced from their home. The need was great. The only help we were able to obtain was from Church World Service.

Our college students volunteered to survey the community, and each refugee family was issued a form. Once that was completed, we could begin distribution. We gave out clothing, rice, flour, bulgar wheat, oatmeal, and powdered milk. We made arrangements with a local bakery. For each five bags of flour the baker used, one bag of flour was given him for his cost. With the flour, nutri-buns were made. Each contained a pint of milk. Each bun was slightly larger than a hot-dog bun, high in nutrition and quite tasty.

One of the distribution days happened to be Carole and my wedding anniversary. The four of us, Carole, John, Marguerite, and myself, spent the entire day helping refugees. It was the best anniversary we have had—a time of mixed joy and sorrow. Words cannot describe the feeling you get when you help someone who is in desperate need and knows you have made a difference in their life. Likewise, one cannot adequately relate the pain that is felt when the supplies run out before all have been served. Their cries, "Help me," still linger in my memory. I wonder if God is bothered by those cries as God waits for us to act?

Conference

Matthew 5:9: Blessed are the peacemakers, for they shall be called sons of God.

At the annual meeting of the Mindanao Conference at Kidapa-wan, I asked to address the conference. In light of the conflicts, which were occurring all over Mindanao, I urged reconciliation with our Muslim neighbors. I tried to point out the similarities between the faiths—that we both worship the same God and we both hold Jesus in high esteem. My efforts were met with modest response.

After I had taken my seat, one of the pastors stood up. He described how some Muslim men had raided his village. Since all of the men were away doing their work (and since devout Muslims will not attack women and children), only minor prop-erty damage had been done. However they had lost face. He personally led a counter attack. The Muslim men, assuming that the Christians played by the same rules and not fearing for the safety of their wives and children, hid in the jungle. He then related how they had killed many women and children before setting the village ablaze. He was met with loud applause. O God, forgive us!

Rebels

John 14:27: Peace I leave with you; my peace I give to you; not as the world gives do I give to you. Let not your hearts be troubled, neither let them be afraid.

October 21, 1972. We had been under a questionably called martial law for just over a month, and the Muslim population was in a state of unrest. They didn't trust the Christians in Manila who ran the country. On three previous Saturday nights, arsonists had destroyed major portions of our city and it was Saturday again. We had planned to make an early start to Iligan City for our weekly shopping but were fortunately delayed.

As we started down the road, armed men came running up a cross street. Every route was blocked. Carrying rifles, knives, and home-made shotguns, several hundred insurgents had crossed Lake Lanao by boats and quickly occupied the city. Intense gunfire sounded from the far side of Marawi City, in the vicinity of the military camp. By 9 A.M. 90 percent of the 40,000 residents had fled the city. Most of our staff had stood outside to watch the events. We consolidated the Dansalan College staff into four dwellings and opened our main building to house refugees. By evening, about fifty persons, both Muslims and Christians, had taken shelter in Laubach Hall. Our clinic, open, treated several wounded from both sides. The night was punctured by the staccato music of automatic weapon fire. We kept the buildings dark and moved close to the floor. We slept quite well. When you are assured that you are precisely where God wants you to be, you lose your fear.

Marawi Bridge

Psalm 91:5: You will not fear the terror of the night, nor the arrow that flies by day.

Early Sunday, the air had a eerie silence. The gunfire had ceased. John and I walked through the nearly deserted city, seeing occasional victims of the fighting. Myrna, who lived with us, was anxious for her sister, who lived near the military camp.

By mid-afternoon, it was still peaceful. So with Myrna, fellow missionary John Hoover, and son John, I piled everybody into our Toyota to look for sister. Her house was secure. Neighbors said they were safe. Then, gunfire returned.

Our hasty exit took us nose to nose with an armored car, which was responding to the gunfire. Turning aside, we discovered ourselves next to the military camp and driving between the combatants. To re-enter the city, we needed to cross over the river. A police car with a white flag waving sped passed. Several men were frantically trying to start a stalled car on the bridge. I put our car into second gear and floored it. We passed the car, crossed the bridge, cut around some barricades, and started up into the city. Halfway up the hill, a machine gun began firing at us. A policemen motioned me to hurry. I was hurrying. The bullets whizzed by, inches over our roof. We made the crest and turned the corner. And, as promised, God took care of even the .50-caliber "arrows."

Our Exodus

Psalm 121:7: The LORD will keep you from all evil; he will keep your life. 8: The LORD will keep your going out and your coming in from this time forth

Monday was relatively calm. That afternoon we received news that the road was now open. We would try to evacuate persons in the morning. Shortly after dawn, I was at the Provincial Commander's office requesting permission to go to Iligan. The colonel gave me a blanket authorization to use the road. In five trips, four that day and one the next. I was able to carry out seventy-six persons and belongings to safety in our station wagon!

For our first trip, Dr. Jaime Arogones, a local Christian leader, requested we take his wife and children in the first trip. He would go later. With Carole and our kids and our three students, we headed to the Arogones' home. In a sudden change of plans, he got into the back seat with their seven kids around and on his lap. As we waved good-bye to his wife, a jeep loaded with armed men drove in, intent on assassinating Jaime. Mrs. Arogones safely joined the family about three hours later. Although we saw no pillar of fire or smoke as did Moses, we knew that God was leading our exodus.

Providence

Matthew 6:31: Therefore do not be anxious, saying, "What shall we eat?" or "What shall we drink?" or "What shall we wear?"...

We were stopped by several military check-points as we drove down the mountains to Iligan. Arriving at the empty mission house which had formerly been our home, I unloaded my passengers and headed back up to Marawi for more. Carole opened the house and tried to make people comfortable. She borrowed some large cooking pots from our Lutheran missionary neighbors and then headed to town to buy food. She wondered if she would be able to feed so many mouths. Some had not eaten since Saturday. Something or Some One told her to check the mail. At the post office was a letter from Holland, Michigan. Enclosed was a check from a family in her home church. A note read, "I knew you would be needing this now." God does provide!!

Feeding the Multitude

Luke 9:16: And taking the five loaves and the two fish . . . all ate and were satisfied.

With the money from the check, Carole headed to the market. She knew that both John Hoover and I would be making several trips with our refugees. Buying a sack of rice, a chicken, and some vegetables, she returned to the mission house and made a huge batch of thick chicken soup, nourishing and delicious. As vehicles emptied, hungry people were fed. When the last person was fed, the pot was empty. All were satisfied. Those who ate numbered about one hundred and ten persons. God did it again!

Symbiosis

Psalm 23:4: Even though I walk through the valley of the shadow of death, I fear no evil; for thou art with me; thy rod and thy staff, they comfort me.

Tuesday night we slept on the floor of the mission house. The next morning, I took three sacks of rice to people in Marawi and spent most of the day there, making certain that things were secure. I had my final load of passengers on board and was about to drive back to Iligan when some Muslim neighbors approached me. Was I coming back? How long would I be gone? They were afraid of the military. Several soldiers had been killed in the fighting and the Christians were as prone to blood revenge as were the Muslims. When it had happened elsewhere in the Philippines, the military had used weapons and napalm to completely destroy a village. The soldiers would be afraid to do that here, they argued, if an American Missionary were in the city. I told them I would return the next day.

Thursday, I returned. That evening I was alone in our house with no one to keep me company except John's pet civet, Rascal. There was sporadic weapons fire, but nothing unusual for Marawi. I kept the lights off as a precaution. Glancing out the window, I saw a shadowy figure on our front steps. I soon recognized the shape of a neighbor. He was seated there, home-made shotgun across his lap. Another neighbor, similarly armed, was at the back. They were protecting me as I was protecting them. I slept well. The Good Shepherd's rod and staff were protecting us all.

Anting-Anting

Matthew 18:14: So it is not the will of my Father who is in heaven that one of these little ones should perish.

Many Filipino people are superstitious. For protection from evil spirits, they carry or hang amulets. In the Cebuano language, they are called "anting-anting." You would use a special form of amulet for the evil in question, be it spirits, thieves, or rice birds which devastate crops. Usually, the belief in charms is quite harmless. However, in the days following the fighting, someone provided an amulet to three small Muslim boys. Made of portions of the Quran, it was supposed to make them invisible. With it, they could attack the soldiers with impunity. Even if they should be killed, they would die in the cause of God and their souls would go immediately to heaven, bypassing any judgment. With simple weapons in hand and "protected" by their amulet, they crawled in bright sunlight across a field towards a sentry. Two were killed by the soldier in self-protection.

The third was wounded. The latter bemoaned the fact that he had to live while his comrades were in Paradise. I wonder if God is angry or weeps when adults cause such tragedy to happen to children.

Fear

Psalm 23:4: Even though I walk through the valley of the shadow of death, I fear no evil; for thou art with me; thy rod and thy staff, they comfort me.

Several weeks after the rebellion, we had just brought the Dansalan staff back to Marawi City. I was awakened in the middle of that night by the sound of an aircraft flying overhead. Other than the recent buzzing of the city by military fighter jets, it was unusual to hear or see airplanes in the daytime let alone at night. I recognized the sound as a DC-3/C-47 and that it was circling Lake Lanao. I roused Carole and we went to our front porch. The plane was indeed circling the lake and flying without lights. Was it military? Was it from guerrilla fighters in Borneo? What was it doing? Suddenly, a phosphorus flare attached to a small parachute began drifting down. Its light illuminated the entire lake. The far shore some several miles distant was clearly visible. From the hill behind and a few hundred yards from our house, howitzers opened fire, lobbing their projectiles over our house and into the lake. The plane began dropping bombs, causing sharp concussions when they struck the earth. For many minutes which seemed like hours, the shelling and bombing continued. Finally, it ceased.

Silence prevailed. Before long, a military jeep with a loud speaker blaring drove through the city. The message was both distorted and in Marano, the local language, which we poorly understood. It was not until well after daylight that we understood that the military was putting on a show of force to frighten the population. Knowing our reaction, I would guess that it was successful. We were comforted by each other and by the knowledge that we were where God wanted us to be. We also learned that fear is indeed a powerful force and that a strong faith is needed to overcome it.

Guilt

Genesis 7:7: And Noah and his sons and his wife and his sons' wives with him went into the ark, to escape the waters of the flood.

I wonder if Noah and his family ever felt guilty because they could escape but their neighbors couldn't. Especially after the above incident, Carole and I were burdened with that kind of guilt. At any time we could pick up and go home. But our neighbors were trapped in a dangerous and traumatic situation. It wasn't fair.

Why does God allow some people to live an almost trouble-free existence while others must endure almost constant horrors? Why do we allow it?

Cholera

Matthew 5:29: If your right eye causes you to sin, pluck it out and throw it away; it is better that you lose one of your members than that your whole body be thrown into hell.

In a nearby area, a refugee camp experienced an outbreak of cholera. The number of infected and dying was growing daily. In addition to treating the disease, finding the source was a priority. It was discovered that the camp had only one privy and that was located above a small river. It seemed like a natural way to dispose of human waste.

However, that waste was being consumed by fish, which were in turn caught for food. It was a vicious cycle. By installing sanitary privies, the incident of new cases was halted. Whether it is a sickness of the body, mind, or soul, it is better to address the cause than the symptoms.

Felix

I Kings 3:25: And the king said, "Divide the living child in two, and give half to the one, and half to the other." 26: Then the woman whose son was alive, "Oh, my lord, give her the living child, and by no means slay it."

Felix had lived across the highway from us when we resided in Iligan City. He and John were the same age and size. They were best friends. Together, they played and swam, fished and caught hermit crabs, climbed on the logs and made toys. When it came time for us to return to the States, Felix's mother approached us.

"Please take Felix with you. His chance for a good life here is limited. With you, he can become something. Please take him." We had to refuse. But we marveled at her love. She was willing to give up the child she loved, knowing that she might never see him again, for his well-being. God so loved the world that he gave his son. . . .

Flashback

Psalm 91:5: You will not fear the terror of the night, nor the arrow that flies by day,

We had been back about three months and living in Connecticut. I was called to preach in many churches in a three-state area. Carole accompanied me when she could. One Sunday in Springfield, Massachusetts, as I was recounting our work in the Philippines, she was reliving our experiences. As I was relating about the rebellion, a helicopter passed over the church. Carole ducked under the pew. It was then that we realized the degree to which we had been affected by what had happened.

Needless to say, the Independence Day's fireworks gave us no joy that year. Slowly our minds and bodies recovered. The God who protects the body during traumatic times, also heals the memory and the mind from their effects.

Phillip Watson

Micah 6:8: He has showed you, O man, what is good; and what does the LORD require of you but to do justice, and to love kindness, and to walk humbly with your God?

Among the many excellent professors who have helped me was Dr. Philip Watson. The first day in his theology classes, he would pass out a sheet with twenty-some questions, our final examination. Several of the questions would be included and nothing else. No tricks nor surprises. Know this material and you won't have any problems. God is like that. The Lord has told us what is required of us. We should not have any problems at the time of testing.

End Times

Mark 13:32: "But of that day or that hour no one knows, not even the angels in heaven, nor the Son, but only the Father. 33: Take heed, watch; for you do not know when the time will come."

I've never been worried about end times. The millennium might be a concern if one knew the starting point—Jesus conception, birth, resurrection, . . .? All of these dates are fuzzy on the calendar. Likewise when someone is certain of the time, I relax. It is obviously not then. Rather I try to plan as if I will live forever and try to live as though this is my last day on earth.

Arrowheads

Matthew 7:7: ". . . seek, and you will find . . . 8: For every one who . . . seeks finds. . . ."

Leonard told this marvelous story. Before entering seminary, he was a truck farmer. He and a neighbor were good friends despite the fact that the neighbor chided him for his church activities. "I've never seen any evidence of God," he would say.

One day Len was at his friend's home. Framed on the walls were hundreds of arrowheads. "Where did you get them?" Len asked. After being told that they were found on that farm, Len said, "I have an adjacent farm to yours and I've only found a few. How did you find so many?" The friend replied, "I think arrowheads. When I go out in the morning, I'm thinking arrowheads. When at work in the fields, I'm thinking arrowheads. When I harvest the crops, I'm thinking arrowheads. As long as I keep thinking arrowheads, I find them."

Len then said, "I'm the same way with God. As I go about my daily tasks, I keep thinking God. And as long as I keep thinking God, I find God all over the place."

Eve

I Timothy 4:16: Take heed to yourself and to your teaching; hold to that, for by so doing you will save both yourself and your bearers.

Pastoral ministry is a partnership between pastors and congregations. It is a sharing of knowledge, wisdom, and experiences. As a young pastor, I was enriched by many fine people. Some, such as Eve, ministered to me in a special way. It was not unusual for her to leave a worship service with the words, "I'll have to think about that." Soon I would receive a huge envelope in the mail with products of her thinking. She would sit at her typewriter and record her thoughts and impressions, what caught her attention and items with which she agreed, disagreed or questioned. She always expressed her comments with love and humility. I hope I helped her as much as she helped me. God should raise up in every church at least one saint like her.

Perspective

Romans 14:14: I know and am persuaded in the Lord Jesus that nothing is unclean in itself; but it is unclean for any one who thinks it unclean.

Our organist was a college student and full of fun. One Sunday she changed the tempo and rhythm, but her Offertory was the "Beer Barrel Polka." Carole and I were the only persons to recognize it. Everyone else seemed to think it was just another beautiful church anthem. And it was. Many of the tunes of our hymns were used in bars before they were used in churches. It is all a matter of perspective. How we think makes something clean or unclean.

Amy

Revelations 21:21: And the twelve gates were twelve pearls, each of the gates made of a single pearl, and the street of the city was pure gold, transparent as glass.

Amy was in her eighties and had developed cancer. After my week at seminary, on Saturday morning I would walk down to Amy's daughter's home where she was living. For the next hour or so, I would sit and listen as Amy told me how good God had been to her. I would leave blessed by this saint. Her daughter would thank me for coming. "It means so much to Mother." I would just smile. I wouldn't have missed it for the world. I was with Amy moments before she died. "Bob," she said, "I just saw heaven and it's beautiful." And she closed her eyes with a smile on her face. When I sat with the family discussing Amy's service, they offered to let me borrow Amy's Bible. It was stuffed with clippings she had gathered over the years. They offered her journal to me as well. I merely acted as editor. The resulting service was a reflection of Amy's life. In her life and in her death, Amy was a blessing to me. I saw Christ in a new way through her. I know that heaven is true. Amy said so!

Youth Fellowship

Psalm 71:5: For thou, O Lord, art my hope, my trust, O LORD, from my youth.

The Camden church was blessed by an active Methodist Youth Fellowship. They were a lively group and fun to work with. One Sunday morning three of the young ladies from the M.Y.F. sat in the back corner of the sanctuary during worship. They were whispering to one another continually. As I was delivering the sermon, I thought it was a waste of time for them to be there. I knew that they had heard nothing. That evening the youth group met. One of the girls who had not been to the worship service asked the three about the sermon. The three repeated the entire message almost verbatim. I learned a lesson. Be cautious not to judge on the basis of appearances. You cannot know what is going on inside an individual.

Boy Scouts

John 21:15: When they had finished breakfast, Jesus said to Simon Peter, "Simon, son of John, do you love me more than these?" He said to him, "Yes, Lord; you know that I love you." He said to him, "Feed my lambs."

The Camden church had long been a sponsor of a Boy Scout troop. Shortly after our arrival, the Scoutmaster resigned and I agreed to take over. I had been an Eagle Scout myself and benefited from the program. Our troop varied from six to ten boys. I'd worried about two Scouts in particular. They were brothers from a very poor family. Their home was a small, non-insulated structure with a dirt floor and space heater in the living room. In the winter a glass of water left overnight in the boys' bedroom would be frozen solid by morning.

One day the younger brother was in the parsonage. Our home was an old farm house, which was on its third church. One church had been condemned and torn down; another was destroyed by fire, and now the present structure. He looked around and said to Carole, "My, what a beautiful home you have."

The Troop had raised the money, and I took all of the boys to Camp Teetonkah. We cooked at the campsite rather than eating in the mess hall. At the end of the week, we were cleaning the cook box. Reusable items were returned to the commissary. The others were trashed. There was an opened almost full quart bottle of white syrup. I indicated that it should be dumped. The same boy looked at me with a sad expression. "I like Karo syrup," he said. I told him he could have it. Opening the bottle, he sat down on a log and drank its contents. Wiping his mouth, he said with the biggest smile I had ever seen on his face, "My, that was good." Whatever form your ministry takes—pastor, teacher, friend, Scoutmaster, neighbor, . . . it feels good to help God feed his lambs.

Assumptions

Matthew 6:9: Pray then like this: Our Father who art in heaven, Hallowed by thy name. 10: Thy kingdom come. Thy will be done, On earth as it is in heaven.

He lived on the opposite side of the church from the parsonage. His wife was a member and active in the life of the congregation. I knew him fairly well, but he had never attended worship. One day he appeared. Afterwards I asked him about his experience. He said that he was angry, embarrassed, and frustrated. He would never come back unless we made some changes. I asked what those would be. He said that he had never learned the Lord's Prayer and had no idea what a Gloria Patri or Doxology was. Why weren't the words printed in the bulletin for people like himself? How often do our assumptions that "everyone knows" concerning things in worship or in the church discourage others from a life of faith?

Priorities

Matthew 6:33: But seek first his kingdom and his righteousness, and all these things shall be yours as well.

They were an affluent young couple with two sons and were members of the church. We had invited them over for dinner. While Carole put finishing touches to the meal, he and I were talking in the study. He noticed our "travels map" on which those journeys that Carole and I have made together are marked.

After studying it for some time, he remarked that he'd give anything to have been all the places we had been. To that I responded. "You have a new Buick and a sports car, a home priced in the hundreds of thousands, and a yacht on the Connecticut River. Would you trade those for my map." No, he wouldn't.

Jesus speaks often of priorities. God makes some very generous offers, but we have to discard some of our present stuff to accept them.

Revealed

Matthew 10:26: So have no fear of them; for nothing is covered that will not be revealed, or hidden that will not be known.

Because of painful experiences while on furlough in Connecticut about being different, when we arrived back in Michigan, both John and Marguerite resolved not to tell anyone of their background. When asked where they came from, they would answer "Connecticut." Their facade went well until one evening when John was at some friend's home watching a James Bond movie on the television. It involved a boat chase on the klongs in Bangkok. John was engrossed in the film. When Bond rounded one turn, John shouted out, "Right up here is a baby elephant." "You've seen this film before," they accused. "No," he replied. "But I've seen the baby elephant."

When the film was over, John and his friends walked down to our house. We got out the slides. They were in awe as they saw Marguerite and John standing on either side of the same baby elephant. Word was then out about their past. Sooner or later, people will discover who you really are.

Prayer

Luke 11:2: And he said to them, "When you pray, say: 'Father, hallowed be thy name. Thy kingdom come . . .' "

Father Howard Murray was the Catholic priest in New Buffalo. Being the only full-time clergy, we were both present at most community events. One would give the invocation and the other the benediction. Howard had been raised in the Baptist church. He was a young adult before he joined the Roman Catholics. In the Philippines, a country where over 90 percent of the population is Catholic, I had learned that in offering a prayer to begin and close with the Trinitarian formula. Everyone will be with you. So there we were Fr. Murray and myself. I, the Protestant, beginning and ending my prayers, "in the name of the Father and of the Son and of the Holy Spirit. Amen." And he would close his with "in Jesus' name. Amen." It is not the how of prayer that counts, but the Who and the do!

Christmas Eve

Psalm 144:15a: Happy the people to whom such blessings fall!

New Buffalo was the larger of the two congregations and hosted any special events, including the joint 8:00 P.M. Christmas Eve worship. When I suggested an eleven o'clock service, they weren't interested. So I approached Lakeside. "We always go to New Buffalo . . . no one will come . . . it's extra work for you . . . okay if you really want it, but no one will come."

At New Buffalo there were about forty persons. At Lakeside where Sunday attendence was less than twenty, over one hundred persons celebrated Christmas Eve. New Buffalo requested the later service for the following year to no avail. When blessings are offered, if you don't accept them, the chances are that someone else will.

Seder

Luke 22:15: And he said to them, "I have earnestly desired to eat this passover with you before I suffer."

For us Holy Week is incomplete without the Seder, the Passover meal. It is the primary root for both Christian and Jewish worship. Anna was a member of our church. Her husband Henry was Jewish. They celebrated the major festivals of both faiths. Henry was in a nursing facility with Alzheimer's. At our first Lent in the church, I asked Anna to be the mistress for the Seder. With tears she recalled memories of Seders with Henry and his family. When Henry died, the family presented me with Henry's yarmulke (skullcap). I wear it each Seder and have carried it with me to the Holy Land. It reminds me of my

Jewish friends such as Henry and Jesus and our common bond in a single meal.

Easter Sunrise

John 20:1: Now on the first day of the week Mary Magdalene came to the tomb early, while it was still dark, and saw that the stone had been taken away from the tomb.

I have concluded that a vegetarian meatloaf is a misnomer, a bowl of chili that did not contain chilies is just a bland stew, and that an indoor sunrise service is an ordinary worship at a horrible hour. But an outdoor Easter sunrise service, especially if it is conducted in a cemetery, is a wonderful and moving experience. The location is important. If we tend to assume that Jesus was only resting, in a trance or in a coma, the grave markers are there to remind us that he was stone cold dead.

Through the years we have had sunrise services on Easters that were balmy, the sun came up like a giant red ball, and we were serenaded by birds in the trees above us. There were others when the skies were as black and dreary as the hearts of the early disciples as they made their way to his tomb. On other occasions the ground was covered with snow and the wind was as bitter as Jesus's experience on the cross. But in each and every situation, there was the joy and the excitement as the words, "The Lord is risen" were met by the resounded echo, "The Lord is risen indeed!"

Cherry Pie

Luke 24:35: Then they told what had happened on the road, and how he was known to them in the breaking of the bread.

Like the disciples on the road to Emmaus, we are all affected by our experiences. My mother was an excellent cook. When she made cherry pie, she pitted her own cherries. My father claimed that when she was finished pitting them, she threw a handful of seeds in with the meats. You ate her cherry pies carefully while waiting for a stone to get you. I still eat cherry pie with caution.

I personally distrust creeds. They tend to divide those who believe them entirely from those who don't. I prefer to talk of experiences. "I experience God as . . ." My experiences will be different from yours, but that's okay. We are different. Creeds may or may not be true. If one accurately shares what was experienced, no matter how unusual that event might have been, the statement is always true. Plus, we are not threatened by differences in each other's experiences. We have lived different lives. We can learn of things that we will never experience ourselves. I will never experience the joy of giving birth to a child. But I can learn from a mother. I can tell of cherry pies. By sharing our experiences, differences become a blessing to all.

Tongues

James 3:8: but no human being can tame the tongue—a restless evil, full of deadly poison.

The kitchen was in the basement of the church and in desperate need of repairs. Many folks from the church met and decided what must be done. Two men volunteered to do the work while donating their time. From the parsonage, which was next door to the church, I saw them working well into the night and almost every night until the task was finished. Even before the dedication could be held, two women from the congregation berated the workers for doing everything wrong. It was many months before we saw the men in church again.

As the sage Thumper says in the movie *Bambi*, "if you can't say somethin' nice, don't say nuttin' at all."

Rabbi

John 3:26: And they came to John, and said to him, "Rabbi, he who was with you beyond the Jordan, to whom you bore witness, here he is, baptizing, and all are going to him."

She was an elderly Jewish woman and the roommate of one of my parishioners in a long-term care facility. She was at a loss at how to address me. I told her that it didn't matter. When I would greet them with, "Good afternoon, ladies," I heard "Good afternoon, Pastor" and "Good afternoon, Rabbi." It's not the words but the intent that counts.

No Comment

Acts 10:34: And Peter opened his mouth and said: "Truly I perceive that God shows no partiality, 35: but in every nation any one who fears him and does what is right is acceptable to him."

The keynote speaker at a symposium on Jewish-Christian relations opened with this story. The rabbi and the minister had houses of worship opposite each other. Although they were good friends, they had an ongoing argument as to whether the Messiah had come or not. Learning that the Messiah was coming, they rushed together to meet him. In one voice they asked, "Is this the first time or the second?" The Messiah looked at both of them with love, smiled, and said, "No comment."

Chain of Command

Matthew 6:9: Pray then like this: Our Father who art in heaven, Hallowed be thy name.

It would be unthinkable for an Army private to make a request of a general. He would have to go through proper channels and up the chain of command.

Many Christians feel that it is unthinkable to go directly to God. But if there is a Christian in heaven with whom they can identify, a favorite saint, the request can be made to them. The saint in turn would pass it on to Mary, who has the loving heart of a mother. If Jesus is going to listen to anyone, it is Momma. He in turn gives the message to General God. It might not be necessary, but it is a comforting option.

Referrals

I Corinthians 7:9: But if they cannot exercise self-control, they should marry. For it is better to marry than to be aflame with passion.

Our kids were in high school. Marguerite has a theology similar to her father's. John has always been more conservative than I am. Therefore it caused us to wonder when he would bring up a conversation at the meal table on the merits of couples living together out of wedlock. He would give his arguments and then ask what I thought. I would respond as best I could. This continued for some time.

Then I started getting the phone calls. "Mr. Pumfery, I am a friend of John's. My girl/boyfriend and I have been living together. John convinced us that we should get married. Can we talk with you?" I did several weddings based on John's referrals. All that many people need to change their behavior is a friend who will tell them that what they are doing is not right.

Vacation Bible School

Psalm 133:1: A Song of Ascents. Behold how good and pleasant it is when brothers dwell in unity!

The annual Vacation Bible School in New Buffalo was a joint effort by the United Methodists, the United Church of Christ, and the Roman Catholic Church. The program was held in the Catholic school, which had the most ample space. Teachers, helpers, and song leaders came from all three congregations. Over three hundred children attended.

The daily closing worship was held in the Catholic church on Monday and Tuesday, and parades with police escort, fire trucks, and all the participants went to the other churches on Wednesday and Thursday. An outdoor worship and picnics closed the activities on Friday. It is amazing what can be done when we set aside our differences and do something together for God and God's people.

Ain't Moved

Psalm 16:8: I keep the LORD always before me; because he is at my right hand, I shall not be moved.

The story goes that an elderly couple was going down the road in their pickup. A young couple passed them, both nestled behind the steering wheel. Ma looked at Pa and said, "Pa, why don't we sit close like that anymore?" Pa replied, "I ain't moved!" When we feel that God is no longer next to us, it is our fault. God ain't moved!

Words

Proverbs 12:18: There is one whose rash words are like sword thrusts, but the tongue of the wise brings healing.

They were a retired couple raising a hydrocephalic daughter. The girl was in her thirties and spent her life in their living room, watching television in the reflection of a hand-held mirror. The mother knew that she was to blame. When she was about five, there had been a death in the family. The body was laid at state in her parents' parlor. Being inquisitive and thinking she was alone, she ventured and touched the body. Just then her mother entered and screamed, "God will never forgive you for this!" As a result at each difficult point in her life, she was certain that an angry God was continuing his punishment for her misdeed.

Why do you and I remember words of condemnation and rebuke from human and often parental voices from the past, while failing to hear words of healing and forgiveness from a heavenly Parent?

The Swamp

Genesis 12:1: Now the LORD said to Abram, "Go from your country and your kindred and your father's house to the land that I will show you."

God has blessed me in the ease of sermon preparation. After I have done the research and other book work, if I can walk in a secluded area, the message essentially writes itself. The problem comes when there is no suitable place for my meditation. This occurred at New Buffalo. We began looking tentatively for some land. About once every three months, I would purchase a copy of the Benton Harbor-St. Joseph newspaper. In an edition in March 1976 was an ad for sixteen acres with swamp, woods, river and springs. We learned later that that was the only day planned for its listing! We called and visited the land.

Carole, John, Marguerite, Carole's and my parents all thought that I was crazy. I offered three-quarters of the asking price and had it immediately accepted. We were land-owners.

We named it The Swamp. In subsequent years, we designed and built with our own hands a house and two-story garage. It has been the site for weddings, baptisms, scores of retreats, and hundreds of hours of mediation and relaxation. For us all, it is home. We firmly believe that God showed us the land, blessed us with it, and asks us to use it as a blessing to others.

Trees

Psalm 134:2: Lift up your hands to the holy place, and bless the LORD!

At the Swamp we have over fifty varieties of trees. Only about a dozen are conifers. The rest, the deciduous trees, exhibit a variety of features during the year. In the spring they exhibit the new growth, with shoots, buds, and flowers. During the summer the rich foliage benefits the surroundings as well as the trees by cooling the air and reducing the evaporation of water from the soils. With the arrival of autumn, the chlorophyll disappears from the leaves, revealing the brilliant reds and golds and yellows, which it had hidden. Then the leaves drop to the ground, revealing what the trees had been doing all along. Like a Jewish man with arms uplifted in prayer, they had been lifting their limbs skyward, blessing their creator.

Stump

Isaiah 11:1: There shall come forth a shoot from the stump of Jesse, and a branch shall grow out of his roots.

Much of the soil at the Swamp is a heavy clay. Because their roots cannot penetrate it, most of the pine and spruce seedlings we have planted have not survived. To maximize our source of Christmas trees, we utilize a technique that a friend taught us. When we first harvest a tree, it is about eight years old. The cut is made above the two or three larger lower branches. By spring, those branches will have turned upwards and begun forming new trees on the same stump. Because the root structure is already developed for a large tree, in a couple of years, they will be ready to harvest.

Judaism and Christianity have both sprouted from the same roots. In our individual faith what, if anything, develops is dependent on the extent and depth of our roots.

Feed My Sheep

John 21:15: When they had finished breakfast, Jesus said to Simon Peter, "Feed my lambs."

Russell and Marguerite were elderly members of our congregation. Everyone loved them and they enjoyed our fellowship. But for them worship was lacking. It wasn't like the Church of the Nazarene where they had formerly attended. I was finally able to convince them to visit a nearby Nazarene congregation. Keep coming here for fellowship, I told them, but please try the other church for worship. They eventually transferred their membership to where they experienced that they were being feed.

Jesus did not say "Count my sheep," but "Feed my sheep!" If we cannot feed them, we should direct them to where they can be nourished.

Blest Be the Tie

John 2:1: On the third day there was a marriage at Cana in Galilee, and the mother of Jesus was there; 2: Jesus also was invited to the marriage, with his disciples.

I have officiated at many memorable weddings—one beneath the coconut palms in the Philippines, a candlelight ceremony in a church decorated for Christmas, our daughter's outdoor wedding at The Swamp. . . .

The most vivid was that of Beth and Chris. A friend of our daughter had brought them to the house to see my model train layout. The next day Beth called. They wanted to get married. She was Jewish, Chris was Catholic. Would I do it? They had met on a steam train excursion and were both "train nuts." We rewrote the service to be acceptable to both faiths. The wedding was held at the nearby LaPorte County Historical Steam Society grounds in the cab of a rebuilt Shay geared logging locomotive. We all wore bib-overalls and engineers caps. The ring bearer carried a specially lettered H.O. gauge gondola holding the ring. The photographer wanted a caption for the newspaper photo. I suggested "Blest Be the Tie That Binds." As individuals and as couples, we are created by God uniquely. We should celebrate that.

Muskegon Heights

I Thessalonians 4:13: But we would not have you ignorant, brethren, concerning those who are asleep, that you may not grieve as others do who have no hope.

Would you consider an appointment to Temple United Methodist Church in Muskegon Heights, asked our district superintendent. The church was in a difficult situation. This could be a six-month appointment, he said. You might be closing up the church. Muskegon Heights is a racially mixed community. The church is a predominately white, middle-class congregation in a poor, predominately black neighborhood. Most members now reside many miles from the church., The current pastor and his wife were in the process of divorce. With his personal life in disarray, the pastor had convinced the congregation that they also were without hope. The best thing, he counseled, was to disband.

I found the congregation discouraged and going through anticipatory grief. For several months I visited extensively and listened closely. Finally, we had a meeting and I shared my conclusions. No, they would never be a "typical" church. No, they would not have an easy time surviving. No, they did not have to close! They voted overwhelmingly to stay. I was there for four years. The church is still serving the community in significant ways. The difference was hope. Without hope in any situation, there is only despair. With hope comes life.

Pain

Jeremiah 8:18: My grief is beyond healing, my heart is sick within me.

I quickly learned that, when an individual or a congregation is hurting, it is impossible for them to see beyond their own pain. It is only as healing takes place that they can become aware of the pain and needs of others. It is then that they can begin to reach out. Patience is needed. Even with God's help, all healing takes time.

Willie Burrell

Proverbs 18:24: There are friends who pretend to be friends, but there is a friend who sticks closer than a brother.

Temple Church had once housed one of the largest congregations in the West Michigan Conference. White flight had seriously reduced the membership. A few year previously, Mission for Area People (MAP) was formed and the forty-plus rooms, including a gym, were well used.

A new director, Willie Burrell, had been appointed and arrived only a couple of weeks before I did. Willie and I worked closely together and became good friends. MAP's program included a community food and clothing bank, GED training, job counseling, youth recreation and training programs, and hosting a senior citizens nutrition site. MAP's board of directors was racially diverse and represented both clergy and lay people from the community. Since it shared the huge building with the church, its major problems were similar, high operating costs and low income.

Together, Willie and I tackled the problems. To keep from losing the senior nutrition site, we obtained funds to install a barrier-free ramp. We then attracted the Headstart program. We battled flooded floors, insect infestations, and frequent break-ins. We commiserated each other over problem people and difficult situations. We encouraged each other. We rejoiced together. Friends working together with God can accomplish much for God's people.

Insincerity

Galatians 2:12: For before certain men came from James, he (Peter) ate with the Gentiles; but when they came he drew back and separated himself, fearing the circumcision party.

I had sensed that one of our black members was having problems with one of our white members. I finally got him to talk about it. He explained that in church on Sunday morning she would greet him like a long-lost friend, being all gushy and sweet. But if he met her in the supermarket during the week, she would not acknowledge that she even knew him.

That is what Paul accused Peter of doing. Does our love for another depend on the setting or who is watching?

Associate Pastor

Luke 14:28: For which of you, desiring to build a tower, does not first sit down and count the cost, whether he has enough to complete it?

We wanted an associate pastor to do race relations work within the black community. The person appointed was a well-educated black man from West Africa, who had studied in the U.S. for several years. In addition to his divinity degree, he held a doctorate in education. He related well with the more educated persons in our community. Willie and I knew we had problems early in the game. We were taking our new colleague on an orientation tour of the inner city areas of Muskegon and Muskegon Heights, where he was expected to be involved.

As we ventured down one of the main streets, our newcomer mentioned that its name, Sherman, was familiar. "There's a Sherman Street in Providence (Rhode Island) too," he remarked. "Do you know who Sherman was?" I asked. He didn't. Nor did he know of Sheridan, Grant, carpetbaggers, Reconstruction, or the Civil Rights Movement. He had heard of Lincoln, but didn't understand the history of the issues. He left after a few months to take a high-paying job with the U.S. government. Our intentions were good. The implementation was faulty. We may have done more harm than good as a result. In God's work, we must take as much care and even more than we would in the business world.

Scoutmaster

Matthew 18:5: "Whoever receives one such child in my name receives me; 6: but whoever causes one of these little ones who believe in me to sin, it would be better for him to have a great millstone fastened round his neck and to be drowned in the depth of the sea."

The Scoutmaster of the troop that was sponsored by Temple church had resigned. I was asked to take over. The troop consisted of fifteen boys from the inner-city neighborhood, all but one of whom were black. Most were living with either their mother or grandmother. Most did not know who was their father. All of them were basically good kids, but almost all would be classified as "at risk."

Pacho was a good example. One day I asked him privately if he knew who his father is. He said that he did. I asked if he lived in the Heights. "No, he's in Jackson." (Jackson is the site of the Southern Michigan Maximum Security Prison.) "Do you get to see him?" "About once a month." "I'll bet he's lonesome." "No, Grandpa's there." Sometimes we cause the little ones to sin by not empowering them to resist evil.

Hospital Chaplaincy

John 11:35: Jesus wept.

The chaplain for Hackley Hospital invited area clergy to be auxiliary chaplains. I was one of the few who responded. For the next couple of years, I covered Tuesday evenings from about six until eleven. My responsibilities included visiting those who just had or were about to have surgery and those in intensive care. In the case of emergency situations, I acted as a liaison between the trauma team and the patient's family. I found that staff often needed my care, especially after the death of a patient. There were many times that I was called upon to console an "aloof and uncaring" doctor, so that he would be able to face the family to inform them that their loved one had died. I wish the families could have seen the tears in the doctors' lounge or nurses station. Only those who do not care are not touched by loss.

Merry Christmas

I Corinthians 16:14: Let all that you do be done in love.

The Christmas Eve service at Temple was at eleven. Since my early evening was free, I went to the hospital to call on patients who had to spend the holiday there. The census was very low. Those who could be, were discharged. Obtaining a list of patients, I set out to call on all of them. Many had visitors, so we just exchanged greetings.

I paused at one room. The patient was alone. When I introduced myself, he said, "You don't want to talk with me." He explained that he was Jewish. I said that that didn't matter and sat down. We talked about many things for almost half an hour.

When I excused myself to go, I wished him a "Good Evening and Happy Hanukah." "Merry Christmas," he answered in a cheery voice. Love is an international and inter-religious language.

Emergency

Matthew 25:41: Then he will say to those at his left hand, "Depart from me, you cursed, into the eternal fire prepared for the devil and his angels. . . ."

One evening following a trauma event in the Emergency Room, the attending doctor told me of an experience he had had some years earlier. A dying man had been brought into the E.R. Nothing could be done for him except to make him comfortable. He was both conscious and cursing a blue streak. When it was suggested to him that he make peace with God, he increased his swearing. Just before his death, the doctor said, he developed all of the symptoms of someone being burned alive. He writhed and cursed and died.

My friend Amy had caught a vision of heaven and died with a smile on her face. Did he have a brief experience with someplace else?

Elephants

Exodus 3:3: And Moses said, "I will turn aside and see this great sight, why the bush is not burnt."

I was driving down I-94 near Benton Harbor, Michigan, when an unusual sight caught my eye. On the north side of the highway were about a dozen elephants in a field. Circus trucks had stopped to allow the animals to exercise and feed. Now every time I pass that spot, I look again in hopes of seeing the elephants.

I wonder if Moses did that with the burning bush. When God puts something special into your life, enjoy it. It might not happen again.

Lord, Help Me

Luke 11:1b: One of his disciples said to him, "Lord, teach us to pray. . . ."

It was a bi-weekly study group. In closing, we were going around the circle with individual prayers. Most of them were nice, flowery, and very proper. That evening we had a newcomer to the group. Prayer/study groups were normally not his thing. He was struggling with many personal problems, including three potentially problematic children.

When it came to him, he said in a voice barely audible, "Lord, help me to be a good father." It had come from the depth of his being and was the most eloquent prayer I have ever heard!

Recognition

John 20:15: Jesus said to her, "Woman, why are you weeping? Whom do you seek?" Supposing him to be the gardener, she said to him, "Sir, if you have carried him away, tell me where you have laid him, and I will take him away."

They had been married for over fifty years. She had been severely ill several times recently. Three times before the doctor had told him that this time she wouldn't be going home. This time she didn't. I met with him and the family in their home across from the church. As we talked about the details of the service, it became apparent that he didn't know his wife—her favorite color, dress, reading material, songs, hymns, Scriptures, flowers, jewelry. . . . I was saddened. It also caused me to wonder. Mary and other disciples had trouble recognizing Jesus in his resurrection body. Do we know our loved ones well enough that we will be able to recognize them in their resurrection body?

Credit

Luke 8:5: "A sower went out to sow his seed; and as he sowed, some fell along the path and was trodden under foot, and the birds of the air devoured it. . . ."

A lady in our church gave me some excellent advice: "It is amazing what you can get done if you do not expect to get the credit!" Once you see what must be or can be done, you start sowing idea-seeds. Many of them will not germinate or take root. But when one does, you water it with encouragement and suggestions. You fertilize it with credit and praise. I have experienced many wonderful crops grown for God this way.

A Special Child

Luke 2:46: After three days they found him in the temple, sitting among the teachers, listening to them and asking them questions.

I had thought that the most difficult parenthood would be of children who are mentally slow. Now I'm not so sure. In our neighborhood was a family whose young son was a genius. Although he was barely in school, he was reading at a high school level. Since our homes were only about a hundred yards apart, he would show up when I was puttering in the yard or garage.

"What are you doing?" "Fixing the car." "What's wrong with it?" "It doesn't seem to be getting enough gas." "Are you working on the carburetor?" "Yes." "What kind of carburetor is it?" "I don't know." "Does it work better than the . . . " The questions continued as long as he was there. Neighbors would rather have door-to-door salespeople come than him. When my patience and tolerance were running high, he'd follow me for hours.

His mother thanked me several times. "He's like that all the time. It's a relief to have him ask someone else questions for a while." I now have new respect for Mary, the mother of Jesus. If at twelve he could spend three days discussing things with scholars, what must he have been like at six or seven?

Attitude

Romans 8:28: We know that in everything God works for good with those who love him, who are called according to his purpose.

In most congregations there are several relatives of Mr. Moan N. Groan and his sister Mrs. Gloom N. Doom. Therefore it is a joy to have someone like Roland and Jean. They had their share of problems. In addition to the normal difficulties of living, there were their medical problems. Of their four children, one son has extreme health problems and another died in college from physical causes. A grandson is severely handicapped.

Although they would acknowledge their pain, I have never heard them complain. To the question "How are you doing," their normal reply was, "We're doing okay. God is good to us." I wish more Christians lived as if they actually believed that.

Pentecost

Acts 2:1: When the day of Pentecost had come, they were all together in one place.

It was in Allegan that I experienced a new miracle of Pentecost. During our ministerial observance of the Week for Prayer for Christian Unity, I challenged our group to show true unity. We often had joint services and events at times like Tuesday noon, etc. What if we could all get together for worship on a Sunday morning at eleven o'clock?

The ball got rolling. Almost all the congregations of the community, except for the sacramental churches, closed their own buildings and gathered at the community auditorium for worship. There were Lutheran and Presbyterian, Reformed and Christian Reformed, Assemblies of God and Church of God, United Church of Christ and United Methodist and a few Episcopalians and Catholics who had skipped mass. When the day of Pentecost had come, WE were all together in one place. I caught a glimpse of what heaven must be like.

Judging

Matthew 7:1: "Judge not, that you be not judged."

She was an older woman. She and her husband lived out-of-town but had begun attending our worship service. Their adult daughter and grandchildren were members of the congregation. One Sunday the theme had been on forgiveness. During coffee hour following the service, she told me that she had problems with forgiveness. When I forgive someone, she said, that means that I have judged them and found them wanting. It is then that I must ask God for forgiveness.

Temptation

Hebrews 4:15: For we have not a high priest who is unable to sympathize with our weaknesses, but one who in every respect has been tempted as we are, yet without sin.

Often when speaking about the fact that Jesus was tempted as we are, someone will say, "But he didn't really want to do it." We have a friend who makes the most beautiful cakes. So artistically decorated are they that they are works of art. To see one is to be tempted. However if you have ever tasted one, it is a different matter. Using the cheapest box-mix she can find and adding nothing to add moisture, her cakes are roughly a cross between cardboard and sawdust. When you knew who made the cake, it was no longer tempting. Temptation is the wanting to. Everyone is tempted, even Jesus. The secret is saying no.

None?

Matthew 12:30: He who is not with me is against me, and he who does not gather with me scatters.

Most hospitals have some method of assisting clergy to find members of their parishes who have been admitted. One Catholic hospital which I visited frequently had a file box with 3 by 5 cards with the patient's name and room number listed. The card were arranged by church affiliation and divided by index cards. If persons indicated their religious preference as "Protestant," it was filed under "None." Was that interpreted as no church or no religion, I wondered. Or both? By saying "Protestant," we indicate what we are protesting against. But what are we for?

Selling Price

Matthew 26:14: Then one of the twelve, who was called Judas Iscariot, went to the chief priests 15: and said, "What will you give me if I deliver him to you?" And they paid him thirty pieces of silver.

They were an elderly couple who owned a small inexpensive house on a very small lot. Some years previously they had been convinced to sign the title over to their daughter to avoid probate. As both of their health deteriorated, they recalled some good years spent in Arizona at a doctor's suggestion. The low humidity had made both of them feel better.

Maybe it would work again. They decided to sell their home and move. "No," said the daughter. It was her house. They couldn't sell it. Within three months, the mother was in a nursing home. Soon they had a double room there. He lasted a few months. She lingered only a few weeks more. I officiated at both funerals. I wish that this were an isolated accident, but it isn't. Of course it is scriptual. It's just the price is higher now.

Shame on Life

Psalm 90:10: The years of our life are threescore and ten, or even by reason of strength fourscore.

When I met her, she was several years past her one hundredth birthday. Her mind was alert and active. The sad part was that she was also blind and deaf and for the most part immobilized. She was a prisoner in solitary confinement within her own body. In addition I have had many persons in nursing homes who have said to me, "Why is God angry with me? Why can't I die?"

There is a story about Gautama who was to become the Buddha. Tradition has it that he was isolated from normal experiences. Then on successive days, he encountered a sick man, an old man, and a dead man. In each case he is said to utter, "Shame on life for having illness (old age, death)." I suspect that it is not the age or the infirmities, but the isolation from family and other loved ones that transforms old age from a blessing into a curse.

Repent

Acts 26:19: "Wherefore, O King Agrippa, I was not disobedient to the heavenly vision, 20: but declared . . . that they should repent and turn to God. . . ."

I enjoy bow hunting, perhaps most by going out in the woods on warm, autumn late-afternoons. I am little threat to the deer. I have two "theological" problems. First, my orientation is often wrong. I need to repent. The word does not mean feeling sorry, but to turn around and face the right direction. My second problem is that I "sin," a word that means "missing the mark." In other words, I need to repent and stop sinning.

To be successful in hunting or in serving God, one must face the right direction and aim precisely at our target. Incidentally, one's aim gets better with practice.

Sex

I Corinthians 7:9: But if they cannot exercise self-control, they should marry. For it is better to marry than to be aflame with passion.

I was new at bow hunting. As I stood in the brush fence-line adjacent to a low area in a hay field, a buck approached and began browsing about forty yards off. Too far for a good shot, I thought. Besides, I was certain that he would see me and be spooked. I would wait. He was soon distracted by two does. I loosed an arrow, which struck the ground a couple yards short of its target. He hardly noticed. Over the next half hour, he chased the elusive does and returned. I got two more arrows off. One landed between his legs. He was fortunate that I wasn't a better shot.

This illustrates what Paul was talking about. Don't be so distracted by sex that you ignore more vital matters.

Letting Go

Isaiah 26:4: Trust in the LORD for ever, for the LORD GOD is an everlasting rock.

I was up north deer hunting and sitting in my blind when I saw something move. About eight feet away, a weasel wearing his ermine coat was starting up a tree. He was completely white except for the black tip of his tail and his coal-black shining eyes. He quickly went up the right side of the tree and disappearing from my view around behind it.

Then I saw what the weasel was hunting. A small mouse clung to my side of the tree, a few inches higher than the weasel.

Letting go, the mouse fell to the ground and scampered to another tree some four feet away from the first. The weasel went up and down and finally left without catching his prey. The mouse was sitting in a knot hole in the second tree, shivering but safe. Letting go was what saved him.

There are times when we cling tightly to an idea, way of action, job, thing or person, all to our own peril. The only way for us to be safe is to let go and trust God.

Generations

Genesis 9:3: Every moving thing that lives shall be food for you; and as I gave you the green plants, I give you everything.

Kalamazoo Valley Community College offered a course that caught my interest, so I enrolled. It was educational, challenging and fun. At the time I was about fifty. There was one classmate a few years my senior, but the remainder were less than half my age. The class met in mid-morning. I would arrive early, get a cup of coffee and a sweet roll from the cafeteria, and review my notes. Several of my classmates did similarly, with a notable exception. They ate potato chips and Mountain Dew. We looked askance at each other concerning our breakfast choices.

About the same time, an elderly widower in our congregation was being pestered by an adult daughter about his eating habits. He enjoyed having supper with friends in a local fast food restaurant. Thinking he should be having something more nutritious, each evening she would call him and question what he had eaten. He finally came upon with a solution. "I had meat and potatoes, lettuce and tomatoes, bread and milk." She was pleased. He had had the usual—a deluxe hamburger, French fries and a milk shake. One generation's tastes and needs in food, music, worship style and many other things may not be like that of the generation before or after.

Special Scouts

Joel 2:28: And it shall come to pass afterward, that I will pour out my spirit on all flesh; your sons and your daughters shall prophesy, your old men shall dream dreams, and your young men shall see visions.

I was asked and accepted a position as Scoutmaster for a group of "boys" from the development center. There were six young men in their early twenties. We met for an hour once a week. We spent about six weeks working on the square knot. "Right over left, left over right." I doubt that it ever held.

During this period, "Wonder Woman" was on evening television. One of my Scouts was caught up in the image. Suddenly in class he would become Wonder Woman and begin spinning to release the special powers. I realized that the difference between men and boys is not only the price of their toys but also the content of their dreams.

Accident

Genesis 2:24: Therefore a man leaves his father and his mother and cleaves to his wife and they become one flesh.

He had been working on a farm when he was caught in a grain auger. His right arm was amputated in mid-forearm. He and his limb were rushed to a hospital and reattached. It was there, but would it function? About three years later, I officiated at his wedding. When it came time for him to light the unity candle, he removed his candle with his left hand, transferred it to his right, and with his bride they lit the central candle. There was not a dry eye in the church. God works through humans to do some marvelous things.

Dogmatic

Mark 10:11: And he said to them, "Whoever divorces his wife and marries another, commits adultery against her; 12: and if she divorces her husband and marries another, she commits adultery."

The atmosphere in my office was too somber for a couple in love. As we talked about their upcoming wedding, he related his sadness. At eighteen he had mistakenly married. Within a few months, he divorced. Now he had found the right person.

However, his grandfather was a Baptist preacher. Because of the divorce, Grandpa had told all of his family not to attend the wedding. He added that if he were in prison for the worst possible crimes but had not previously been married, they would all be there. At the wedding, none of his side came. How often do we trample on love in the name of Jesus?

Meagan's Baby

Acts 16:33: And he took them the same hour of the night, and washed their wounds, and he was baptized at once, with all his family.

Theologians often debate the pros and cons of the various modes of baptism. I have long suspected that variation occurred because of compassion. Was it the crying mother with the sick baby or perhaps the dying saint without enough water for immersion that started a particular form?

Meagan was about three when her parents brought her for baptism. I had talked with them previously and during the ceremony. I explained to Meagan (and the congregation) what was happening. She was eager to be an official Christian. During the baptism, Meagan clung to a doll she was holding. As the family was returning to their pew, Meagan came running back to me. "My baby wants to be a Christian too!" I felt Jesus smiling as we consecrated Meagan's baby.

Ellen

Genesis 12:2: And I will make of you a great nation, and I will bless you, and make your name great, so that you will be a blessing.

Our church wanted to hire someone from the nursery during church school and worship but didn't want to take anyone away from their own church. Ellen was selected. She was a nineteen-year-old college student who attended Saturday evening Mass at the Catholic church next door. Ellen was bright, up-beat, and outgoing with a continual smile. She loved kids and dreamed of becoming an elementary teacher. She volunteered at the library and the snack bar at the hospital. Then cancer intervened.

Over the next couple of years, she underwent numerous surgeries, leaving her without stomach or bowels. We talked often about her fear and her faith, trust and doubt. She knew the intimacy of God's love and presence but confessed he often felt distant. After a close call with death, she confided to Carole that she didn't understand why she was going through this, but that she wouldn't change a thing. So many good things had happened, she had met so many wonderful people, she had learned so much, and God had really blessed her.

Ellen knew that she was dying and that very soon she would be with God in heaven. But she was no longer afraid. She was trusting, expectant, and even joyful. Less than half an hour before Christ came to take her to the spiritual kingdom, Ellen was singing, laughing, and smiling. I was privileged to deliver her eulogy at the Catholic church. I remarked that a depth of faith like Ellen's is rare. But being a blessing to others is not dependent upon age.

Doxology

Colossian 3:16: Let the word of Christ dwell in you richly, teach and admonish one another in all wisdom, and sign psalms and hymns and spiritual songs with thankfulness in your hearts to God.

Since earliest times familiar secular songs have provided the tunes for Christian hymns. In 1989 when the University of

Michigan won the national basketball championship, I wrote the following Doxology to the tune of "The Victors."

Hail! to our God, our Father,
   Hail to His Christ, our brother,
Hail! Hail! to God in us,
   His Spirit of love.

Hail! to His Church Triumphant,
   Hail! to his loyal people,
Hail! Hail! His kingdom reigns,
   On earth and heaven above!

TLC

John 19:27: Then he said to the disciple, "Behold your mother!" And from that hour the disciple took her to his own home.

It was a second marriage for both, and they had recently retired. Word came that his three oldest grandsons, who had been removed from the home of his daughter from his first marriage, were in dire straits. Their adoptive mother had been killed in an accident. The father couldn't take care of them. They went to see the boys. Her reaction was immediate. We have to take them home and raise them. For the next several years, this couple who should have been enjoying the leisure of retirement were raising three teenage boys with emotional problems. Their faith and tender loving care worked wonders. I wonder what troubled persons are out there waiting for my or your faith and TLC to work with God in a transformation in their lives?

Rabbits

Matthew 24:41: Two women will be grinding at the mill; one is taken (snatched) and one is left. 42: Watch therefore, for you do not know on what day your Lord is coming.

My father taught me how to catch wild rabbits with my bare hands. When they are sitting in some cover, they believe that they are invisible and cannot be seen. Once you spot them, it is fairly simple thing to approach them from behind and snatch them with a quick grab. It is taken. Many people are like those rabbits. Somehow they assume that God cannot see them and know what they are doing. But then. . . .

Paul

Romans 8:28: We know that in everything God works for good with those who love him, who are called according to his purpose.

Paul was a retired nursery-man in his seventies and a member of our congregation. He was a hard worker with the motto, "I would rather wear out than rust out." Because of some fatigue, he visited his doctor. A stress test and angiogram indicated a need for by-pass heart surgery. Wanting a second opinion, he visited a well-known medical center, which recommended just medication. Just go home, they said, and resume your normal activities. They didn't know Paul.

He started the next day by splitting some rock by hand for a retaining wall he was building. He then dropped a couple of trees, cut them to length, and split them with a sledgehammer and wedge for firewood. After lunch, he picked up his shotgun and walked a couple of miles to his favorite spot for some deer hunting. At supper he remarked to his wife that he had just had his best day in several years. That night he suffered a fatal heart attack. I think God heard and answered.

Statues

Exodus 28:12: And you shall set the two stones upon the shoulder-pieces of the ephod, as stones of remembrance of the sons of Israel.

Many years ago her late mother was a spiritualist minister in Illinois and purchased two statues that were being removed from a Catholic church. St. Francis and St. Joseph came to Michigan with the family. Her father was moving to smaller quarters and no longer had room for his tall, silent companions. He had been to The Swamp and loved our place. Would we house them? Frank and Joe, complete with tabernacle bases, now grace our home? We all need objects of remembrance for a life of faith.

Habitat

Matthew 25:40: And the King will answer them, "Truly, I say to you, as you did it to one of the least of these my brethren, you did it to me."

My introduction to Habitat for Humanity came with an invitation from some parishioners. They were going to northern

Michigan to work on a house. Did Carole and I want to go? The new homeowner was a woman in her forties who worked at a local grocery store. She and her wheelchair-bound daughter lived in the shack across the street. It was little more than a few sheets of plywood and some tar-paper. She was radiant with joy in the prospect of the Habitat home. In the practice of Habitat for Humanity, it was a modest, affordable, well-built home. In her eyes it was a palace. We helped on a couple more homes in that area before being appointed to Three Rivers.

Habitat was still in the talking stage there, so I jumped in. I served on the Board of Directors for our entire stay, with stints as vice-president and president. Being a small affiliate, we built only one home a year. But with each house, one family moved from sub-standard housing into their own home. I discovered once again that doing beautiful things for God can be addictive.

Razi

John 8:11: And Jesus said, "Neither do I condemn you; go, and do not sin again."

Shirazi Dream, Razi for short, is our cocker spaniel. He is generally well behaved. But when he is untied and sees a squirrel, rabbit, cat, or other small animal, he is off and running. Our shouts of "No!" are of no avail. He will return with head down, knowing he has done wrong. I will say, "Razi, Razi, Razi, what will we ever do with you?" Then I pat him on his head and all is well. Isn't that how God treats us? I do what I know is wrong. I come to God with my head down. And God says to me, "Pumfery, Pumfery, Pumfery, what will we ever do with you?" Then he pats me on the shoulder and I know all is well.

Eclipse

I Corinthians 13:12 KJV: For now we see through a glass, darkly;
but then face to face: now I know in part; but then shall I know
even as also I am known.

The moon covered most of the sun, leaving only a crescent
visible. The light coming through the leaves of the maple tree
left bright, moon-shaped images on the patio. I had the camera
out, with filters and other attachments to cut down the amount
of light so that I could view and photograph safely. The full
glare of the light could damage the eyes. Scripture tells us that
God is light and to look upon God will cause death. Is it because
of God's brilliance that we must look "through a glass darkly?"

Honor

Mark 6:4: And Jesus said to them, "A prophet is not without
honor, except in his own country, and among his own kin, and
in his own house."

He was absent from our worship service a couple of times a
month when he was speaking on behalf of the Gideons. One
day he came to me and said that he was withdrawing his membership. When asked why, he explained. When he was in other
churches, they gave him all sorts of honor and respect. But here
they just treated him like everyone else. After he left our
church, he neglected to worship elsewhere. Soon he stopped
and resigned from Gideons. How often our pride gets between
us and God.

Balance

Ecclesiates 1:9: What has been is what will be, and what has been done is what will be done; and there is nothing new under the sun.

The symbol for the Taoist faith is the yin-yang. It is the familiar circle divided equally into the two tadpole-shaped halves, one black and the other white. The yin is feminine, dark, cold, damp, north, negative, passive,. . . . The yang is masculine, bright, hot, dry, south, positive, active, . . . The whole of anything is incomplete with just one. A balance must be attained between the two.

As modern psychology touts its new notion of right brain/ left brain and the need for balance between the masculine and feminine attributes, the Taoist sage must be observing with a knowing smile.

Limiting God?

Isaiah 55:8: For my thoughts are not your thoughts, neither are your ways my ways, says the LORD. 9: For as the heavens are higher than the earth, so are my ways higher than your ways and my thoughts than your thoughts.

He was a likable man who did not attend church, although he had when he was growing up. His wife and children were moderately active. In time he shared his experience. He had been in the military in Vietnam. His commanding officer had ordered him to walk a group of enemy prisoners several miles back to base and for him to return alone in ten minutes. He understood and obeyed. Now he was overwhelmed with guilt.

He could not forgive himself. Therefore, God, he knew, could never forgive him. We would never dream of limiting God's power to what we can do. Why do we try to limit God's forgiveness?

Darwin

Romans 8:28: We know that in everything God works for good with those who love him, who are called according to his purpose.

When we first met Darwin, he was in his late fifties and an active member of the congregation. He had lost his right arm just below the elbow as a child, had had major cancer surgery to his face and neck several years before, and recently had been forced to retire from his office job because of Parkinson's disease. He rejected the concept of handicapped. He had won state archery championships in competition against two-handed men and women. His garage was lined with trophies from gun and bow. He farmed, cut wood, and lived an active life. His positive attitude is an inspiration to all who know him. "Handicaps" are too often a state of mind.

Matthew

Matthew 13:13: This is why I speak to them in parables, because seeing they do not see, and hearing they do not hear, nor do they understand.

Carole, our son John, his wife, Virginia, grandchildren Jason, Aaron, Nicci and Matthew and I were having a deer drive with Darwin in his woods. Matthew was about eight at the time and was easily distracted. Observing something near his feet, he paused to look. He failed to see a deer, which jumped up less than six feet in front, bolted past him, and barely missed a collision. How often are we engrossed in something minor and miss the truly dramatic gifts of God, even when they almost run us down?

Raccoons

Proverbs 13:16: In everything a prudent man acts with knowledge, but a fool flaunts his folly.

Raccoons were getting into everything. Plus they left their droppings on every flat surface. I had had it. Carole and I had just retired for the night when a censor light flicked on. Being sure that it was a raccoon, I grabbed a shotgun and went out. I slipped around the house in the darkness. Another step would trigger another light and I would have it.

In the blaze of light, I saw in our firebowl seven little raccoons about the size of grapefruit. I couldn't shoot. Getting Carole we watched and photographed them. One sniffed my knee. When we went to bed, I knew that our problems had just multiplied by seven. When emotions prevent you from taking decisive actions, the problems generally don't go away. They just grow. But often compassion makes them more tolerable.

Miracle of Ears

Acts 2:4: And they were all filled with the Holy Spirit and began to speak in other tongues, as the Spirit gave them utterance.

I have come to believe that the real miracle at Pentecost was not in the speaking but in the hearing. Many people of different languages understood in their own tongue what the apostles said. It has happened to me scores of times that someone will approach me with, "Rev. Pumfery, you really helped me in this week's sermon when you said . . ." They will then quote me. What they heard is not what I said. That's an example of the miracle of ears. God has a wonderful way of taking what has been said and transforming it in the ears of the listener into what that person needs to hear.

Two Churches

Matthew 5:23: So if you are offering your gift at the altar, and there remember that your brother has something against you, 24: leave your gift there before the altar and go; first be reconciled to your brother, and then come and offer your gift.

In northern Indiana, there are two churches close to each other. One is of modest size, about fifty years old and sturdily built of brick. It is of a mainline Protestant denomination. The other is smaller, perhaps fifteen years old and is of questionable quality wood construction. It bears the name, "Church of the True God." I suspect they were once one congregation. And then he said and she said and . . . Jesus surely didn't mean that we had to be reconciled with people like that before we could worship, did he?

Father Bob

Psalm 133:1 A Song of Ascents. Behold how good and pleasant it is when brothers dwell in unity! 2 It is like the precious oil upon the head, running down upon the beard, upon the beard of Aaron, running down on the collar of his robes!

We were looking for an organist when we found a newspaper ad by an organist looking for a job. A publishing error gave the wrong number. But another ad was for organ lessons with one digit difference in the number. We hired Bob. His mother had been raised Methodist. His father was Catholic, and Bob was baptized as such. Although he attended parochial schools, his maternal grandparents took him with them to church. He became a priest and was now on leave. Bob and I became good friends. Our mutual greetings on Sunday were, "Good morning, Father." "Good morning, Pastor." When I was gone, Bob filled the pulpit. On the first Sunday of the month, I served him communion. It is good when brothers dwell in unity!

Why?

Psalm 22:1 My God, my God, why hast thou forsaken me? Why art thou so far from helping me, from the words of my groaning?

He was seventeen, bright, outgoing, fun-loving and very likable. He had been a member of the youth group, confirmation class, and a guest in our home. He had been our paper boy. Most of all, he was our friend and we expected great things from him. The church had helped rescue his older sister from an abusive situation in their home, but he insisted that he was okay. Then one afternoon he killed his parents. Three lives were wasted

—theirs and his. At the parents' funeral, my message was based on part of the above verse. "My God, my God, why?" Did someone, did we, did I fail them? What did we miss? Who else and what else are we overlooking? My God, my God, Why?

Jennifer

John 14:12: "Truly, truly, I say to you, he who believes in me will also do the works that I do; and greater works than these will he do, because I go to the Father."

With the risen Christ at work in our world, people have done some amazing things. At a check-up for an ear infection, a physician spotted a growth in our youngest granddaughter's eye. The retinal blastoma was only a millimeter away from the optic nerve. A gold plaque the size of a bottle cap was notched to fit around the nerve, scored and the grooves filled with radioactive material. Her eyes was popped out, the plaque sown to it, and the eye reinserted. Five days later it was removed. The tumor was killed. When I look at Jennifer, I thank God for empowering mankind to do great works!

United

Matthew 6:11: Give us this day our daily bread; 12 And forgive us our debts, As we also have forgiven our debtors; 13 And lead us not into temptation, But deliver us from evil.

In 1942 the Grace Methodist Church and the First Congregational Church merged to form the United Church of Ovid.

Through the years most of the pastors have been from the United Methodist Church and only one from the United Church of Christ. As a result, the congregation leans toward the Wesleyan side of the family. In the Lord's Prayer, "trespasses" has been used, while those from the Puritan branch wanted "debts." To most people, "trespass" is what you do on someone's property while "debts" conjures up images of credit cards and banks. In united spirit we now use "sins." "Forgive us our sins as we forgive those who sin against us." No one has any doubts what that means.

Neighbors

Leviticus 19:18: You shall not take vengeance or bear any grudge against the sons of your own people, but you shall love your neighbor as yourself: I am the LORD.

The storm struck early morning with sustained winds in excess of ninety miles per hour for over ten minutes. Scores of trees in our community were broken or uprooted. Thousands of limbs littered the ground. Wires were down. Streets were blocked. Despite a population of only 1,600, within a couple of hours, over 200 volunteers were out with trucks and chainsaws and front-end loaders. By dark, all streets and driveways were cleared and trees were removed from vehicles and buildings. But of more importance, strangers became neighbors and neighbors became friends!

Pruning

John 15:2: *Every branch of mine that bears no fruit, he takes away, and every branch that does bear fruit he prunes, that it may bear more fruit.*

Most plants do best with periodic pruning—removing that which is dead, unfruitful, or that which hinders the growth of the plant. Sometimes it is done with forethought and deliberation. Occasionally it is cause by a wind or gale. Unfortunately, a storm removes some of the good along with the other.

I have discovered that God allows the winds of the Holy Spirit to blow through the doors of the church. At times it is a gentle breeze, which warms and refreshes. At others it like a hurricane causing turmoil and uprooting. When the dust clears, some members will be gone and sorely missed while the absence of others will benefit the congregation. After the healing is done, growth resumes. Often with more vigor.

Grief

Psalm 77:10: *And I say, "It is my grief that the right hand of the Most High has changed."*

Whatever the loss—a pastor, member, building, etc.—a congregation experiences grief as do individuals. We had been helping one congregation with its pain for more than a year. Then one Sunday morning, an older lady of the church walked into the sanctuary before worship. Looking around, she remarked, "Bob, I hadn't noticed how we've let the church deteriorate." It was a good sign. A woman (or church) that is very ill will not care about her appearances. It is optimistic when she replies to your comment about how well she is looking, "How can you say that? My hair's a mess and I don't have any make-up." Healing takes time. But God will help to change an individual's or a congregation's grief into joy.

Listen

Matthew 18:21: Then Peter came up and said to him, "Lord, how often shall my brother sin against me, and I forgive him? As many as seven times?" 2 Jesus said to him, "I do not say to you seven times, but seventy times seven."

Whatever the grief situation, those experiencing it do not want explanations, advice, or even extended words of comfort. They want someone to care about them and someone to listen to them—about how things were, what happened, and what they are feeling now. You may have to listen to an individual a dozen times and a congregation for a dozen times the number of members. It is as Jesus told Peter about forgiveness: you keep doing it until it is no longer necessary.

Anger

Matthew 18:21: Then Peter came up and said to him, "Lord, how often shall my brother sin against me, and I forgive him? As many as seven times?" 22: Jesus said to him, "I do not say to you seven times, but seventy times seven."

A bullet often kills through impact. Blood loss can be secondary. As the Rabbi's knife to the throat of an animal causes the blood to flow externally, the arrow works internally. The longer that the razor-sharp point is within the wound, it keeps cutting. In much the same way, as long as we keep anger within us, it keeps slicing. The resulting pain, infection, and festering robs us of strength and dims our outlook on life. The arrow shot at us by someone else does them no discomfort. While an animal can seldom dislodge an arrow, we can rid ourselves of the arrow of anger through forgiveness. We must seek to remove it, even seventy times seven times, until we are freed from its influence and healing can begin.

Columbus

Genesis 50:20: As for you, you meant evil against me; but God meant it for good.

The Greek classics were saved from being lost when the great Caliph Harun al-Rashid had them translated into Arabic in the eighth century A.D. When it came to Ptolemy's scientific compendium, the Caliph had the accuracy of each entry verified. By the second century B.C., several scientists had calculated the circumference of the earth to almost the exact value. Ptolemy, however, had a figure approximately two-thirds the correct amount. Two scientists were asked to check Ptolemy's figure. With the tools necessary for the task and a large amount of money, they set off.

A couple of years later, they returned and said that Ptolemy was right! Later a young Christopher Columbus studied Ptolemy in the university. By knowing the distance to the east coast of Asia, it was simple arithmetic. Japan was only 3,000 miles west of Lisbon. If the two deceitful scientists had done their job, it is doubtful that Columbus would have ever sailed. God has a marvelous way of turning evil deeds into good results.

Being Fed

Luke 9:11: And taking the five loaves and the two fish, he looked up to heaven, and blessed and broke them, and gave them to the disciples to set before the crowd. 17: And all ate and were satisfied.

There is the story of a man who had a vision of hell. Hungry people sat around a table laden with food. Each had one hand tied behind their back and a long-handled spoon attached to the other so that they could not get the spoon to their mouth.

He then saw heaven. The scene was the same except that the people were laughing and well-fed. They were feeding each other. I have observed that those who are busy spiritually feeding others are never those who complain about not being fed.

Hidden Treasure

Matthew 13:44: "The kingdom of heaven is like treasure hidden in a field. . . ."

There is a statue of the Buddha in Bangkok with a fascinating story: Following World War II, a huge concrete statue of the Buddha was found in the Thai jungle. No one knew its origin. It was plain and ordinary. Should it be left where it was? Deciding that it should be moved, its weight was calculated and an appropriate size lift crane brought in. It was a few feet off the ground when the boom broke and statue fell and split. Inside was a two and a half ton solid gold statue of the Buddha. The monks had hidden it with concrete before the advancing Japanese army. Probably they had been killed protecting their secret. No one knew what treasure was hidden inside. We all know some rather ordinary people, books, communities and churches. What wonderful treasure has God hidden within them?

Angkor Wat

Matthew 6:19: "Do not lay up for yourselves treasures on earth, where moth and rust consume and where thieves break in and steal."

In the Cambodian jungles is the temple complex of Angkor Wat. It had been lost for centuries. As we viewed the magnificent structures and intricate artwork, something very simple caught my attention. There was a large stone wall. Each stone was about five feet long and three feet in both height and depth. Rain had made small pockets on the surface of one such block. In one pocket, a seed had caught and produced a tree. The roots of the tree had slowly and gradually split the stone block. The work of many men had been undone by a tiny seed. Nothing we do is permanent. Only God is eternal.

Style

Luke 10:41: But the Lord answered her, "Martha, Martha, you are anxious and troubled about many things; 42: one thing is needful."

We were waiting at a train depot in Japan. If John, three, wasn't walking, he was generally on my shoulders. Carole carried Marguerite, one, on her back in the African style—with one leg on either side of Carole's waist. As we waited for our train, a Japanese woman approached with a small boy on her back in the Japanese style—with his legs downward. The two ladies eyed each other. Using gestures they debated the relative merits of the two styles carrying children on the back. There were many laughs and the shaking of the head "no." How often do we get into needless anxiety because we have not sorted out what is needful and what is simply a difference of style or opinion?

Namaste

I Corinthians 3:16: "Do you know that you are God's temple and that God's Spirit dwells in you?"

The common greeting in India is a posture with head bowed slightly in deference, hands clasped with palms together as if in prayer and the word "namaste" is said, meaning "I bow to the divine within you." I like that. We say that we believe that God dwells in the heart of each believer. I wonder how our lives would change and the lives of others if we acted as if that were true?

Retirement?

Matthew 6:31: Therefore do not be anxious, saying, 'What shall we eat?' or 'What shall we drink?' or 'What shall we wear?'" 33: But seek first his kingdom and his righteousness, and all these things shall be yours as well.

I was on a study seminar in India. One of our resource people was Mr. J. P. Misra, a teacher and a devout Hindu. He was at the age when many American men would be thinking of retirement. His children were grown. He had substantial savings put aside. And indeed he was looking toward the future. He had made arrangements that his wife would be well cared for. In a few years, he would leave his teaching position and life as he had known it. Going to a wilderness area, he would live as a hermit and work on his soul. His concern was not what he would eat, drink, wear or be sheltered, but his spiritual condition. I am reminded that "retirement" is not a biblical concept.

Varanasi

Revelation 22:1: Then he showed me the river of the water of life, bright as crystal flowing from the throne of God and of the Lamb.

Before our bus trip to Varanasi, Mr. Misra explained to us the significance of what we would visit. Varanasi is a confluence of seven rivers, two are physical and five are spiritual. Mr. Misra went on to explain that this water is the purest on earth. He maintained that this could be proved by biological and chemical analysis.

One descends to the river past a long line of pilgrims asking for alms. Temples (ghats) line the bank, along with hostels for pilgrims and priests. The aroma of wood fires fill the air as the smoke from cremations hangs low in the air. Worshippers are at the water's edge or standing in the stream itself. Many carry small brass pots with which to take home some of the precious liquid for anointing, much like Christian pilgrims will do from the muddy Jordan. The Ganga (Ganges) is very wide at this point and appears highly polluted. Objects float in the brown current. Some distance out, sea eagles devour the floating carcass of someone or something.

Then I looked at our guide and friend. He was experiencing something that I could not. He watched the crystal-clear water flowing from the abode of the gods, sparkling as it carried its refreshing and healing essence. It is only those with the eyes of faith who glimpse the richest visions.

Lazarus

Luke 16:19: "There was a rich man, who was clothed in purple and fine linen and who feasted sumptuously every day. 20: And at his gate lay a poor man named Lazarus, full of sores, 21: who desired to be fed with what fell from the rich man's table; moreover the dogs came and licked his sores."

India is a wonderful and depressing country. In it I had seen Christ in the beggars and in the lepers, in the homeless and the hungry, in the sick and in the dying. While on the bus between Lucknow and Varansai, I realized that I had met my Lazarus. I wrote the following, with the tune of "O for a Thousand Tongues to Sing" in mind.

O Christian, do you hear their voice?
    They cry aloud to you,
"Reach out your hand, give me your love,
    God's love is for me too."

The ragged woman with the bowl
    of cow-dung on her head;
her life's as precious as is yours,
    to save her life, Christ bled.

Behold the sick man on the ground,
    his body full of sores;
like Lazarus before the gate,
    the gate for him is yours.

The begging child that follows you
    cries, "Give Bakhsheesh° to me!"
O Christian, please don't e'er forget
    Christ's grace for you was free.

The hungry, naked, sick and poor,
    all cry aloud to you.
for Christ has given you the task
    his work on earth to do.

So let us join and vow to God
    that we'll his will obey,
and serve his children as did Christ
    in every place and way.

°alms

Taj Mahal

Luke 12:20: But God said to him, "Fool! This night your soul is required of you; and the things you have prepared, whose will they be?"

Shah Jahan had a dream of two beautiful tombs across the river from each other. The first would be a glistening white marble for his wife. The second of black marble for himself. Her mausoleum was completed, and she now rests within the Taj Mahal. Only the foundation for his was completed when he died. His dream died with him. His mortal remains were placed next to his wife. We cannot assume that our children (or anyone else) will buy into our dreams.

Calcutta

Matthew 5:43: "You have heard that it was said, 'You shall love your neighbor and hate your enemy.' 44: But I say to you, Love your enemies and pray for those who persecute you, 45: so that you may be sons of your Father who is in heaven;"

Calcutta is a mispronunciation of Kali Ghat, the temple of Kali. Kali is a multi-armed, black goddess who wears a necklace of human skulls. Animal sacrifices are still offered, with their blood thrown on her image. On the day I visited the temple, a garland-bedecked corpse lay on a stretcher in front of the entrance. A large toe of this deceased worshipper had been removed and offered to Kali.

A short distance away is the mother house of the Sisters of Charity. It is here that we spent almost an hour with Mother

Teresa, a person who simply radiated Christian love. What a contrast between two admired women. If you loved them, both would be gracious in their love and embrace. If you were an enemy of Kali, she would hold you in her embrace as she terminated your existence. If you were an enemy of Mother Teresza, she would still embrace you with love and treat you as a friend. That's what sets Christians apart. They'll know we are Christians by our love.

Salvaged

Acts 2:21: And it shall be that whoever calls on the name of the Lord shall be saved.

One of the terrible sights of India is the Rag Pickers, those desperate individuals who sort through the garbage to find something that might be salvaged. There might be some food or a piece of clothing or . . . The word "salvaged" comes from the same root as the word "saved." If Jesus had lived in India, perhaps John would have written, "I am the good Rag Picker. Whoever calls on me will be salvaged."

Eldest Sister's Day

Proverbs 31:28: Her children rise up and call her blessed; her husband also, and he praises her: 29 "Many women have done excellently, but you surpass them all."

In America we celebrate Mother's Day because we think of "mother" as being the one who gives us our primary nurture and care. In India it is the eldest sister. With many families on the brink of starvation, mother is too essential in the work force to be saddled with child care. That task falls to the oldest daughter, who becomes a surrogate mother. She will forgo schooling and even marriage until all of her siblings have been raised. To honor her, Eldest Sisters Day is an annual and major event. Whoever gives us the tender loving care we need is worthy of honor.

Reincarnation

Matthew 7:13: "Enter by the narrow gate; for the gate is wide, and the way is easy, that leads to destruction, and those who enter by it are many. 14: For the gate is narrow and the way is hard, that leads to life, and those who find it are few."

There is an almost universal belief in a life after death. In most religions, there are qualifications. Sort of a qualifying examination. For Christians, Muslims, and Jews, it is a one-shot proposition. If at the end of your life you are in tune with God, you are in. If not, you fail. The Hindus and Buddhists believe in multiple chances. If your soul does not measure up in one life, your soul is reincarnated in a form that will best help you meet your deficiencies. This is repeated until you do pass. If at first you don't succeed, try, try again.

Enlightenment

Ephesians 3:20: Now to him who by the power at work within us is able to do far more abundantly than all that we ask or think, 21: to him be glory in the church and in Christ Jesus to all generations, for ever and ever. Amen.

It was in the heat of the day when I strolled alone from the guest cottage to the temple. Nothing was stirring. The smell of dust was in the air. Distant cattle crowded under sparse shade. Ahead of me, benches encircled an ancient banyan tree. It is said that it had sprung from the roots of the one under which Guatama, the Buddha, had sat and was enlightened. It was a very holy spot.

I sat there for an hour or so in meditation. It was a memorable time. No, I was not enlightened at that time. Spiritual experiences do not depend on external conditions but internal ones.

Lepers

Mark 1:40: And a leper came to him beseeching him, and kneeling said to him, "If you will, you can make me clean."

We were touring Bethany Village, a colony for persons with leprosy and their families. There persons with leprosy were enabled to become economically independent and to achieve self-esteem and public respect.

Two men caught my attention. The first sat idly in a corner bemoaning his fate. The disease was in check, but he had lost part of one foot. Life was miserable, he told us. Everything was difficult and the future looked hopeless. We were moved to pity. But then we met the second man. He had lost all of his fingers and his eyesight. But he had a broad smile and was singing hymns as he turned out yarn on a spinning wheel. It is not what life does to you, but what you do with it.

Well

Matthew 10:42: And whoever gives to one of these little ones even a cup of cold water because he is a disciple, truly, I say to you, he shall not lose his reward.

The village's well was like a huge cistern from which water was drawn and into which sub-surface water seeped. As the summer progressed, the water table lowered and the well wouldn't be replenished. A mission project targeted that well. Holes were made in the rock with jackhammers. Dynamite was inserted and ignited. About six feet of rock was removed from the floor of the cistern. Now the well will not run dry and the little ones shall receive their cup of cold water. Blessings.

Thomas

John 14:5: Thomas said to him, "Lord we do not know where you are going; how can we know the way?" 6: Jesus said to him, "I am the way, and the truth, and the life; no one comes to the Father, but by me."

On the southwest coast of India is the city of Cochin, where there is a substantial Jewish community and an ancient synagogue. It is also the site of the headquarters of the Mar Thoma Syrian Church. The apostle Thomas arrived here about 52 A.D., preached at the synagogue, and founded the church. I was impressed by their loving spirit and generosity. Although the rule is that half of all moneys given to the church must be given away, in practice it acts as a minimum not a maximum.

An example is their work in the Cochin slums. The church purchases a lot and builds a house. After selecting the most desperate family, regardless of religion, the house is given to them and the process starts again. They also have homes for the elderly and for the orphans. Above all, they have love. From Thomas, they have learned to walk the way, know the truth and live the life.

Doubters

John 20:29: Jesus said to him (Thomas), "Have you believed because you have seen me? Blessed are those who have not seen and yet believe."

Thomas crossed the tip of Indian to Madras and founded another congregation. After visiting China, he returned to Madras. About eight miles southwest of the city center is a high hill

198

called St. Thomas Mount. The metropolis now surrounds it. It was there that Thomas lived, met with the new Christians, and prayed.

One day while in the midst of his meditation, Thomas was pierced through with a spear and died. A huge cross was erected on the site. Today in that predominantly Hindu city, that cross is visible from virtually every point in the urban areas. When airplanes arrive or depart, they must circle around the cross. All of this because of a man whom much of the world had dubbed The Doubter. I wish all of our congregations were filled with doubters like him!

Food

I Corinthians 10:17: If one of the unbelievers invites you to dinner and you are disposed to go, eat whatever is set before you without raising any question on the ground of conscience.

While living overseas I developed a philosophy about food. First, it is a gift of God. Second, there is nothing that you can eat for which there is not a pill that will correct things. Third, to refuse to eat something can be a blatant insult to someone else (suppose someone refused to eat your mother's favorite dish because it looked "gross"). Fourth, if you do not eat the specialties of an area, you are missing a potential blessing (as would someone who refused to eat fresh strawberry shortcake on a spring visit to southwestern Michigan).

On our India Seminar, many of my companions were afraid of almost everything. Fortunately I found two kindred spirits. Spring and David were p.k.s (preachers kids) in their late teens. "What's that?" they would ask. "I don't know," I would answer, "but it smells good. Let's try it." Together we were blessed by many foods and delicious tastes, which the others missed. We were also among the few with no digestive complaints during the entire five weeks. For the last night of the seminar, we were divided into groups of three or four to eat in Indian homes. All but the three of us ate in Westernized Christian homes. Spring, David, and myself were invited to a high caste Brahmin home, where we sat on the floor, ate from common bowls with our fingers, and had a fantastic experience. As Paul adds, "So, whether you eat or drink, or whatever you do, do all to the glory of God."

Cancun

Matthew 6:21: For where your treasure is, there will your heart be also.

When John graduated from high school, we asked him what he wanted for a gift. He answered, "To go some place where I can swim in warm, salt-water." Together with Ginny, whom John would eventually marry, our family spent a week at Cancun, Mexico that summer. Although our nights were spent in a deluxe hotel, our days were spent away from the resort areas. Our meals were taken where the locals eat. We were impressed with contrasts. The villagers were poor, but smiles, singing, and laughter were prevalent. The tourists were very wealthy by comparison but exhibited very little joy. Too often stuff gets in the way of life.

Breath

Genesis 2:7: then the LORD God formed man of dust from the ground, and breathed into his nostrils the breath of life; and man became a living being.

For our twenty-fifth wedding anniversary, we traveled to Quito, Ecuador, to visit friends who were missionaries at HCJB. High in the Andes, it is a Christian radio station, which broadcasts programs around the world. After our time with them, we spent a few days in Peru. From Lima we travel by train to Huancayo on probably the most amazing rail trip in the world. At one point we were well over fifteen thousand feet in elevation. A porter carrying a large plastic bag filled with oxygen passed through the passengers cars offering anyone who was light-headed to inhale from the container. We chuckled. One puff might clear your head for a few seconds, but there would be no lasting effect.

As I thought on this, I reflected on how this is like the experience of many Christians. In both Hebrew and Greek, the word for "spirit" also means "wind" and "breath." Many Christians have experienced being filled with the Holy Spirit, the Breath of God. That's great. But like the bag of oxygen, one gulp is not sufficient. A newborn baby's first breath is good. If it doesn't keep on inhaling, that's bad. The Spirit of God is as available for us to take in to our souls as air is for our lungs. To inhale once is a good beginning. Living occurs only when it happens repeatedly and habitually.

El Nino

Luke 2:7: And she gave birth to her first-born son and wrapped him in swaddling cloths, and laid him in a manger, because there was no place for them in the inn.

We had visited a weekly market with its two miles of stalls in the morning and were to tour Huancayo in the afternoon. Our guide said she had something more interesting. We drove to a nearby community of Huayucachi for their El Nino fiesta. The soccer field was surrounded with sellers' booths. Bands were playing. In the crowd were a few dozen masked men in ancient Spanish military uniforms, some red and some blue. A strange soccer match was in progress with the reds versus the blues. The participants' vision was obscured by the masks.

Then the main attraction began. A circle about twenty feet in diameter was drawn on the field. A timekeeper with a stop-watch, a referee, and two judges with clipboards stood nearby. A red and a blue, each carrying a bull-whip, would enter the ring. A whistle was blown. For the next thirty seconds, they lashed at each other, blows being recorded by the judges. Then two more, etc. In the end, one side had tallied the most blows and was declared a winner. They and their supporters then snake-danced out of the field and into the town. The fiesta reflects a military engagement between Spanish conquistadors Pizarro and Almagro at Christmastime in 1538. It is an unusual feature of their celebration of the birth of The Boy-Child. What are yours?

Angels

Genesis 28:12: And he dreamed that there was a ladder set up on the earth, and the top of it reached to heaven; and behold the angels of God were ascending and descending on it!

Not everyone believed in angels with wings. We have inherited that image from the Greeks. In the Scriptures, the seraphim, the cherubim, and other creatures have wings. But angels generally are wingless.

A cathedral in Lima, Peru, has an interesting example. The Spanish Catholic priest hired native artisans to do the statuary for the church. Jesus and the Apostles resemble Incas. When it came to the angels, the priest explained that they were messengers between God and humans and that angels had wings. The sculptors placed the wings on the back of the head! How wise they were. Angels help to wing our thoughts and prayers to God.

Exchange

2 Corinthians 5:20: So we are ambassadors for Christ, God making his appeal through us.

The World Methodist Council has an exchange program whereby a pastor from one country will exchange roles with the pastor from another. Most of these are for a month duration and involve an exchange between a pastor from the U.S. and one from the British Isles. I exchanged pulpits with Ken Russell from Whangerai, New Zealand. With the distance involved and cost of travel, ours was for six months. In his words, we "swapped everything but our wives." We lived in their house, used their dishes, drove their car, and served his congregation, St. John Church. It was a great experience for both pastors and both congregations. We shared ideas and cultures. Most of all, as all Christians are called to do, we shared Christ.

Aotearoa

Matthew 16:2: Jesus answered them, "When it is evening, you say, 'It will be fair weather; for the sky is red' . . . You know how to interpret the appearance of the sky, but you cannot interpret the signs of the times."

The Maori name for New Zealand is "Aotearoa," "The Land of the Long White Cloud". The ancient Polynesians were expert navigators, despite the fact that they had no maps, written records, or even the crudest instruments. What they did have was an awareness of the behavior of clouds.

Clouds normally drift across the sky. But the high islands of the Pacific are nearly always wreathed with stationary clouds, caused by the moisture-carrying trade winds being cooled by the elevation. Such a cloud on the horizon would indicate an island, even several sailing days in distance. Once such an island has been discovered, it can be returned to by sailing in the same general direction and watching for the tell-tale cloud. In the case of New Zealand, the long white cloud. Today we have devices and gadgets, which we have learned to depend upon. As a result, we have lost the ability to read many of the signs. I suspect that we have also forgotten how to read the messages that God has placed there for us.

Environment

Isaiah 43:18: Remember not the former things, nor consider the things of old. 19 Behold, I am doing a new thing; now it springs forth, do you not perceive it?

When the Maoris arrived in New Zealand, there were no mammals and few reptiles. Without natural predators, many birds had become flightless. The Maoris brought rats, dogs, and pigs. Europeans would bring cats, deer, Australian opossum, hedgehogs, hares, etc. The hedgehogs have been a blessing by eating snails and garden pests. The opossums have destroyed millions of trees, while the cats and dogs have made many birds extinct. The introduction of foreign elements has drastically changed the flora and fauna of the land.

Similar situations occur in religions. When Christianity moved out of Palestine, it left a Semitic world and entered a Greek one. The ways of thinking and viewing the world were very different. Each new region, culture, and age had its own indigenous faith-species, which affected the whole to a greater or lesser degree. Some were beneficial. Others were detrimental. But they are all became part of the present Christian scene. Just as the environment of the New Zealand, which the Maoris discovered, is gone, so is the Christianity of Jesus' Apostles. Both changes might be deplored, but we can't go back. The original is lost forever. We can only go forward.

Origins

Galatians 3:28: There is neither Jew nor Greek, there is neither slave nor free, there is neither male nor female; for you are all one in Christ Jesus.

The two main islands of New Zealand are separated by a narrow strait. It is interesting since the two are of different origins. The North Island is geothermal, with volcanic cones dotting the landscape, geysers, and the like. The South Island is tectonic and created by the interaction of two plates of the earth's crust. The southern island has rugged mountains, fjords, and glaciers. They are different in origin, structure, and appearance. What if people with as unlike characteristics as these two islands could coexist peacefully side by side?

Tui

Acts 2:15: For these men are not drunk, as you suppose, since it is only the third hour of the day.

The tui is an indigenous New Zealand songbird about the color and size of an American blackbird, but having two distinctive balls of white feathers at its throat. The tui especially enjoys nectar from certain flowers, fruits and berries. On a visit to a nature preserve, we observed tuis in a tree eating small fruits, which had begun to ferment. The tuis were drunk! They sang loud and long. They staggered, fell, and had difficulty in getting up. They were impervious to their surroundings. All that interested them was the source of their inebriation. They appeared disgustingly human. How much better to exhibit intoxicated behavior because you have drunk of God's Spirit.

Harrier

Matthew 24:44: Therefore you also must be ready; for the Son of man is coming at an hour you do not expect.

The harrier is a marsh hawk from Australia that has immigrated to New Zealand. Like many people the harrier seems to adopt the attitude that bad things are those that happen to someone else but not to me. The harriers find the road kills along the New Zealand highways as convenient sources of food. As a vehicle approaches, the harrier will often ignore it until the last moment. It was not uncommon to see a dead harrier lying next to the remains of a dead opossusm. It wasn't ready. A common admonition of the New Testament is "be ready." We will all face difficult times, including death. If we have developed a faith and relationship with God, we will not be run over and crushed by them.

Easter

Luke 14:16: But he said to him, "A man once gave a great banquet, and invited many; . . . But they all alike began to make excuses."

Being south of the equator, April in New Zealand is roughly equivalent to October in North America. Lent is when the days shorten rather than len(gh)ten. Easter is an autumn holiday and has become similar to our Labor Day. It is the last long weekend of summer. It is time for the final trip to the cottage or beach, to get the boat in from the water and enjoy the fading rays from the sun. It provides excellent rationales for staying away from

207

worship. Church services see their lowest attendance on Easter Sunday. How does that rank with the excuses we make?

English?

Isaiah 33:19: You will see no more the insolent people, the people of an obscure speech which you cannot comprehend, stammering in a tongue which you cannot understand.

It is not only an obscure speech and stammering tongue that can cause problems. It has been said that America and England are divided by a common language. We found that problem in New Zealand and South Africa as well. For example, cupcakes are called "cookies," cookies are called "biscuits," and biscuits are called "scones." "Tea" in the morning and afternoon means just that. But "tea" in the evening means supper. On the other hand, "supper" means a late meal or bedtime snack. Or, dealing with vehicles, if you are driving your lorry (truck) and get a puncture (flat), you remove the tyre with the spanner (wrench) and fetch the spare from the boot (trunk) or under the bonnet (hood).

The list goes on. Communication is always a challenge regardless of the language or with whom you are sharing. But it is always worthwhile with others and with God.

Casket

Romans 6:23: For the sages of sin is death, but the free gift of God is eternal life in Christ Jesus our Lord.

If you were to attempt a New Zealand crossword puzzle and needed a six-letter word meaning "a small box or chest as for jewels," you would probably struggle before coming up with "casket." The British writers told of pirates who would find a deserted island on which to bury their treasure casket. In Australia and New Zealand, the term "casket" also denotes the prize offered in a lottery. "Buy a ticket and win the golden casket." If one equates gambling with the sin of failing to trust in God to provide, then the term "casket" is all the more fitting in both usages of the word.

Operating Instructions

Deuteronomy 6:6: And these words which I command you this day shall be upon your heart; 7 and you shall teach them diligently to your children. . . .

It was mid-May and therefore late fall in New Zealand. A friend had invited Carole and me to the government farm where he was research director. They were trying to develop sheep that would have their lambs in the autumn. Christmas is a high demand season for lamb. An autumn-born lamb would be four months older, large and more profitable for the farmers.

As we were touring the facilities, our friend noticed a ewe having difficulties in giving birth. Soon he and Carole were acting as midwives. Finally the lamb was born. It was on the grass almost lifeless. With encouragement, the ewe began licking her newborn. Shortly the lamb was standing on wobbly legs and following its mother around the paddock. In a few weeks, it would be independent of her and able to exist on its own.

How different that is from a human child. We are virtually helpless for our first half dozen years, and most of us are not ready for self-support until we are three times that age. It is the responsibility of the parents that the child is raised safely and properly.

Fortunately God has provided us with "operating instructions." The Law provides us with the "manufacturer's guidelines" for optimum performance. God does not say that it is impossible to do otherwise. But if we don't do so, problems will develop. When we follow God's directions religiously, we have the best opportunity for abundant living.

Rainbow

Genesis 9:16: When the bow is in the clouds, I will look upon it and remember the everlasting covenant between God and every living creature of all flesh that is upon the earth.

New Zealand is a wonderful place for observing rainbows. We had frequent brief rain showers, followed by bright sunshine. It was not unusual to see half a dozen rainbows in one day. On the two-hour trip down to Auckland one day, we saw over twenty and drove through three! Rainbows occur when bright sunlight passes through tiny water droplets. Acting like a prism, the light is broken up into an infinite range of colors from ultraviolet through the blues, greens, and yellows to oranges and reds and finally infra-red. Each color contains an authentic portion of that original white light. It is only when all of the colors are combined back together that the complete character of the radiation is re-established.

I like to think of the rainbow as being much like God's presence with people. God is light and allows that light to shine upon us. Human character acts like the prism or water droplet. God's light is divided into an infinite number of colors, and each individual shines with a different color. As we gather together, our composite hue changes. It is only when we all get together, each reflecting the light that he or she has received, that we can return the original pure radiation to God.

Jerusalem

Luke 19:41: And when he drew near and saw the city (Jerusalem) he wept over it.

Our first two visits to Jerusalem were when it was a divided city with a no-man's land running next to the King David Hotel. Our guide on the initial trip was a Palestinian Christian and himself a refugee. His account of the evacuation was that the British informed them that they would have to leave their homes for fifteen days. They could take nothing with them—no money, no clothing, no furniture, nothing. After all, they would be right back. If they did take something, they would be shot. That had been thirteen years before.

He took us to a place where we could see his home. He had watched Israelis wearing his family's clothing and using his furniture. He wanted to go home. People who had lived in Jerusalem for thirteen centuries were displaced for people who had not lived there for nineteen centuries but wanted to go home. For the city called holy by three major religions that worship the same God—Jews, Christians, and Muslims—God must still be weeping.

Damascus Gate

Psalm 100:4: Enter his gates with thanksgiving, and his courts with praise! Give thanks to him, bless his name!

Our Israeli guides had carefully steered us away from Muslim places of worship and Arab businesses. One afternoon at the hotel, I was approached by a young Arab shopkeeper who had recognized me from a previous visit. Would I bring my group to his store in the old city that evening? We had made plans to go to Ben Yehuda Street in the new city but agreed to meet him by the Damascus Gate later. He met us at the appointed time and escorted us down the dark street to his shop. With the city wall silhouetted against the night sky, the honey-combed dome of the gate mystically visible in the shadows, the shuttered windows with trickles of light making their way through the cracks and the soft sounds of a city going to sleep, it could have been the city of the first century as well as the twentieth. Could the muted voices behind a barred door be those of Jesus and his disciples. If so what was he saying? Perhaps that the Lord who was worshiped in Jerusalem could be found wherever people turned their hearts towards God.

The Upper Room

Matthew 8:14: And when Jesus entered Peter's house, he saw his mother-in-law lying sick with a fever; 15: he touched her hand, and the fever left her, and she rose and served him.

Our group was scheduled to celebrate the Lord's Supper in the Upper Room. One of our ladies woke up with a terrible cold. She contemplated staying in the hotel but joined us at the last minute. Following the communion service she said to Carole, "Did you touch me?" Carole replied that she hadn't. "As I was taking communion someone put their hand on my shoulder and my cold was gone instantly," she said. Somebody touched her while she was praying. It must have been. . . .

Traditions

I Corinthians 11:2: I commend you because you remember me in everything and maintain the traditions even as I have delivered them to you.

Surrounding most sites in the Holy Land, one finds a combination of facts and legends, truths, and traditions. Some persons are disturbed by the unproved statements. For example, in the lower level in the Church of the Holy Sepulcher is a covered well. Tradition has it that when Helena, the mother of the Emperor Constantine, visited there in the early fourth century, she found three crosses in that well.

Suspecting that one was that of Jesus, she had three sick men brought and touched each with a splinter of a different cross. The first died. Obviously, the cross was of the unrepentant thief. The second was moderately improved in health. The cross was of the repentant thief. The third man was cured instantly. She had found the cross of Christ. I approach this tradition much as I do some American ones. George Washington is said to have thrown a silver dollar (before there ever was one) across the Delaware River (which is an impossible feat). If it didn't happen, it surely should have.

Bedouin

Luke 2:7: And she gave birth to her first-born son and wrapped him in swaddling cloths, and laid him in a manger, because there was no place for them in the inn.

As you drive down from Jerusalem to Jericho, you can still see camps of the Bedouin, the nomadic people of the desert. Some have obtained sheets of metal to incorporate into their dwellings. Other use tents and natural formations, such as caves and rock shelves for shelter. In the winter months, the animals join humans in houses, tents, and caves for mutual benefit. The animals are protected from the elements while the people are warmed by the heat radiating from their four-footed companions. That is especially valuable for infants.

Like most tribal people of the Middle East, the Bedouin swaddled their newborns. The long bandages with which the child is wrapped provides a confinement, warmth, and security similar to the womb. When we are told that Mary wrapped Jesus in swaddling clothes and laid him in a manager, it is saying that his birth was very ordinary. It happened hundreds of times each year. From the very beginning, Jesus was just like us.

Jericho

Matthew 10:26: "So have no fear of them; for nothing is covered that will not be revealed, or hidden that will not be known."

One of the more popular sites in Palestine is Jericho, where the walls came tumbling down. Thousands of tourists visit it annually. In 1961, when we climbed to look down at the excavations of the ancient walls, our eyes drifted to the north side of the tell. There before us spread a huge refugee camp of Palestinians who had been displaced from their homes by the partitioning. Hundreds of thousands of people were crowded into makeshift houses. At each succeeding visit, there were fewer and fewer homes. The Israeli bulldozers had been busy. The refugees had been moved to where they would not be seen. The Israeli authorities didn't want foreigners to see that they were doing unto others what others had done unto them. Don't we all try to hide our sins, hoping that they will be undetected? But we forget that God always knows and eventually probably most other people will too.

Two Seas

Mark 4:24: And he said to them, "Take heed what you hear; the measure you give will be the measure you get, and still more will be given you."

The Jordan River begins in the foothills of Mount Hermon, between Lebanon and Syria, and flows southward into Israel. Shortly after crossing the border, it empties its precious moisture as well as any minerals it has collected into the Sea of

Galilee near the town of Capernaum. A few miles farther south, it leaves the Sea of Galilee and traverses the Jordan Valley, passing near the city of Jericho and, farther on, the site where Jesus was baptized. Then it empties into the Dead Sea and is no more. The one river feeds two seas. Both receive the blessing of its moisture and minerals.

The first, the Sea of Galilee, does not try to save its gift but passes it on. It is teeming with life and its waters are good. The Dead Sea does not give anything away, but keeps all that it receives. As a result, what began as a blessing turns into a poison. The sea became lifeless. God pours blessings into our lives as well. If we try to hoard them for ourselves, they act as a poison to our soul. If we pass them on to others, we are enriched with abundant life.

Storm

Luke 8:23: and as they sailed he fell asleep. And a storm of wind came down on the lake, and they were filling with water, and were in danger. 24 And they went and woke him, saying, "Master, Master, we are perishing!" And he awoke and rebuked the wind and the raging waves; and they ceased and there was a calm.

I have seen storms on the Great Lakes when six-foot breakers crashed against the pier and huge ore carriers were hesitant to venture out. But I couldn't imagine a storm on a puddle the size of the Sea of Galilee, a mere thirteen miles long and eight miles wide at its broadest, that would threaten a well-built boat. When we had observed it, the sea was smooth as glass. Most tours include a boat ride from Tiberias to Capernaum. On the day we were to go, a strong wind was blowing across the lake and stirring up two to three feet waves. The rain was coming down in the proverbial buckets. We were halfway across when we were informed that we would be landing on the Golan Heights side. The storm had washed out the dock at Capernaum. Most of the passengers, including all of our group, were in the sheltered lower portion of the vessel. I sat on the open deck as the boat pitched and rolled. With the rain and the spray running down my face, I shut my eyes and imagined that I was on the boat with Jesus. In that kind of storm, smaller boats and especially one without power would have troubles. Perhaps two were holding the tiller and fighting to keep the bow into the waves, which splashed into the hold. Do we wake the Master? Finally in desperation, "Master, Master we are perishing!" Then Jesus spoke, "Peace! Be still!" And the wind ceased, and there was a great calm. As I opened my eyes, we were still in the midst of that beautiful storm. But I had gotten a glimpse of the one who could cure the people and heal weather.

Capernaum

John 14:2: In my Father's house are many rooms; if it were not so, would I have told you that I go to prepare a place for you?

Opposite the ancient synagogue in Jesus' adopted hometown of Capernaum is the ruins of a fascinating house. Like many old farm houses in Michigan, you can almost read the family history in the structure. Mom and Dad built it and raised a family. The daughters wed and went to live with their husbands. The sons married and brought their brides home. The house was too small, so they put on an addition. As the family grew and grew, more rooms were added. In the center of that Capernaum house is a courtyard where communal meals were prepared and consumed. Adjacent to it was the original house to which many rooms had been added through time. With this home in mind, I can almost hear The Carpenter saying to us, "Since you are now kin, I'm going on ahead to put an addition on Dad's place so your room will be ready when I come and get you."

David and Goliath

I Samuel 17:40: Then he took his staff in his hand, and chose five smooth stones from the brook, and put them in his shepherd's bag or wallet; his sling was in his hand, and he drew near to the Philistine.

Police often visit the scene of the crime to try to reconstruct the sequence of events. I have never experienced this as vividly as the site of the battle between the Philistines and the Israelites. We stood on a hill on the edge of the Shephelah, the low hills that separate the Judean Hills of the Hebrews from the plain along the Mediterranean Sea where the Philistines lived. The hilltop was strewn with shattered Philistine pottery. Here was a handle from a jug, which Goliath might have used. There was part of a bowl, which might have been broken by David. Facing the east with the land of the Philistines stretching out behind me, I grazed over the "scene of the crime."

At the base of the hill was a rock-filled wadi where a stream flowed after a rain. The stones were ideal for skipping on a pond—rather flat with diameters of two to four inches. Just beyond the wadi was another low hill at the terminus of the Valley of Elah, which sweeps down from Bethlehem.

This was probably the site of the Israelite camp, I could see it easily. David walking from his home in Bethlehem down to the place of battle, the five smooth stones, the fleeing Philistines after the death of their champion and the looting of their camp. When an occurrence can be visualized, it changes from a story into an event.

Arad

II Kings 23:5: And he (Josiah) deposed the idolatrous priests whom the kings of Judah had ordained to burn incense in the high places at the cities of Judah and round about Jerusalem;

In the south of Israel lies the ruins of the fortress city of Arad. Within its walls was a "high place," patterned after the temple in Jerusalem. It is the only known provincial shrine in Judah. In its courtyard were two standing stones, one somewhat larger than the other, and at the entrance to the Holy of Holies were two stone altars of similar proportions. Apparently they were for God and his consort, Asherah. As they say, when people can misunderstand, they (we) will.

Wadi Musa

Numbers 20-11: And Moses lifted up his hand and struck the rock with his rod twice; and water came forth abundantly, and the congregation drank, and their cattle.

Just before arriving at the beautiful rock city of Petra, you come to the village of Wadi Musa. A Wadi is a usually-dry river course, similar to the arroyo in the American Southwest. Musa in the

Arabic means Moses. The Arroyo of Moses. Here in the middle of the Jordanian desert, enclosed by a small mud brick building, is a spring. Ancient tradition has it that this is the biblical Massah and Meribah, where Moses struck the rock. It is said that the flow of water has never ceased. To the Middle Easterner, running water is living water. It thus becomes an illustration of the Rock from which the Living Water never fails to flow.

Damascus

Acts 9:11: And the Lord said to him, "Rise and go to the street called Straight, and inquire in the house of Judas for a man of Tarsus named Saul."

Damascus is a fascinating city. You can walk down Straight Street and enter what is said to be the house of Judas, where Ananias baptized Saul/Paul. We visited a mosque, which had been a church until the tenth century. For almost two thousand years, John the Baptizer has been venerated here by Christians and then Muslims. It is one of several sites that claim to have John's head. It is also said to be the place where Jesus will return. Our Muslim guide pointed to one of the four minarets and said, "There is where Jesus will come back to earth. He will come down that minaret. The bad will be destroyed. The good will live forever." Then he added, "Alhumdulilah" (Praise to God!) Yes, indeed. Alhumdulilah!

The Fib

Proverbs 15:20: A wise son makes a glad father, but a foolish man despises his mother.

My father was an avid hunter. The last trip that he and my mother took together was to Canada for the September bear season. A few weeks later, my mother was taken ill and hospitalized. A few months later, she died. Dad had reserved the same hunting cabin for the next fall. Initially he was unsure if he would return, but by mid-summer Dad had decided he would go again. Carole and I thought it unwise for him to return there alone.

So I told a fib. "Dad, I've always wanted to go bear hunting." Carole added that she wanted to accompany us. For the next seven years, the three of us headed north the first week of September. We had wonderful times together. The last year we went, Dad was eighty-eight years old. He wounded a bear, but we couldn't find it. Six weeks later, Dad died of cancer. Isn't it great how God takes something you do out of the sense of duty and transforms it into a blessing for you and for others.

Signs

John 14:13: Whatever you ask in my name, I will do it, that the Father may be glorified in the Son; 14 if you ask anything in my name, I will do it.

I enjoy reading signs. I have seen "Dead End" and "Rest Area" signs by cemeteries. By a large pile of building scraps was a sign "Instant Homes." Just add water? One day near Wharncliffe in Ontario, I passed a riding stable with the sign "Enter and Ride at Your Own Risk." About a hundred yards farther was a cemetery with the sign "Enter at Your Own Risk." Open graves? Ghouls? Vampires? Perhaps we need signs on the churches, "Pray at Your Own Risk—You May Get What You Ask For."

Honey

Matthew 5:30: And if your right hand causes you to sin, cut it off, and throw it away; it is better that you lose one of your members than that your whole body go into hell.

We were bear hunting in Canada. Our eldest grandson, Jason, had gotten his bear and asked to join me. We had checked the bait in the morning and added some honey. By the time we returned at 3:30, the bear had come and gone. With little hope, we sat in the woods about one hundred yards off and waited half-heartedly. The night before, visibility was gone by 6:30. About 6:25 I started getting stuff together to leave when I saw something near the bait. Apparently we had spooked him when we walked in and he had waited three hours, thinking about the remaining honey. That was his undoing. His snout was sticking with it. Even for us, not suppressing urges can be fatal. Sometimes eternally!

The Way

John 14:6: Jesus said to him, "I am the way, and the truth, and the life; no one comes to the Father, but by me."

I had wounded a black bear, which disappeared into the brush. Bringing our outfitter, he and I began tracking the blood trail. After more than half an hour, we came upon the bear and killed it. After field dressing it, the task was to drag it back to our vehicle. I said it was one way. He said another. I was certain that I was correct, but he "knew the woods." We went his way. After another half hour, he said, "This isn't right." "That's what I've been trying to tell you," I replied. "But it seemed right." Whether it is in the north woods or in living out our lives, following what seems right often leads us in the wrong direction. We need to follow someone who knows or is the Way.